The Many Faces of Faith

My Miraculous Healing from
Dissociative Identity Disorder

A Memoir

Faith Alison & Vivien Chambers

Copyright © March 25, 2024 by Vivien Chambers

All rights reserved.

No portion of this book may be reproduced in any form without written permission from Faith Alison, except as permitted by U.S. copyright law.

Cover design by Vivien Chambers & Jenica Butler
Art design by Vivien Chambers
Art by Thad Foster

Dedicated with love to

Steve & Stan

&

J. Daniel & Becky Smith

Contents

Preface	1
Prologue	3
1. I Want to Die	4
2. Rapha	14
3. Confronting My Parents	34
4. Home	44
5. Letters	60
6. Eating Disorder	78
7. Inner Child	88
8. Chronic Disease	102
9. Different Voices	116
10. My System of Alters	134
11. Maymee Calls Vivien	160
12. A Banquet for Annie	178
13. Forgiving	186
14. Steve Doesn't Get It	208

15. Spiritual Nourishment	226
16. Daphne's Integration	236
17. Children With Jesus	248
18. Total Integration	272
19. Howard	298
20. Cry Out to God	310
21. PhD-Perfectly Healed & Delivered	328
Afterword	336
Acknowledgements	339
Timeline	340
Works Cited	344
About the Authors	345

Preface

Daydreaming is a common form of dissociation. Nearly everyone dissociates at some time or another.

Extreme dissociation is sometimes used to cope with traumatic situations the victim can't physically escape. This can result in a fragmented mind that sometimes assumes the form known as "ego states" often called "multiple personalities." Professionals in psychiatry now call it "Dissociative Identity Disorder (DID)."

According to an article on HealthyPlace.com titled *Dissociative Identity Disorder Statistics & Facts/HealthyPlace*, "Dissociative Identity Disorder has always been considered to be quite rare but it may be more common than previously thought and some estimate it to affect 1% of the population. This higher estimated prevalence may be due to the millions of now reported incidences of childhood abuse."

Many books have been written about people with DID who have somehow learned to manage their psychosis and continue to live with it while some testify about healing. The healing process can be as varied as the individual. The point is, healing is possible. This is the story of Faith's healing process.

Faith's memoir is written in such a way as to invite the reader into her fragmented mind and to experience her healing journey. Much of the text and poetry is derived from her journals. Some topics are categorized rather than chronological to make the story more legible, minor details have been added for enhancement, last names are omitted, and Faith's name has been changed to protect her family. All else is true as perceived by Faith.

Prologue

There is a dimension beyond that which is known to common man. It is the middle ground between light and shadows, between truth and deception, and it lies between the pit of man's fears and the summit of his faith. This is the dimension of the psyche. It is an area which is called Dissociative Identity Disorder.

You are about to meet a suicidally depressed woman.
Witness: Faith Alison, age thirty, occupation: wife, mother, amateur musician, poet, and songwriter.
Afraid of the following: abandonment, failure, disease, responsibility, and life in general.
Present interest: to find eternal peace from mental anguish.
Preoccupation: to end the life of Faith Alison.
One abiding concern about society: if Faith Alison should die, the world would be better off.

This is Faith's Exodus. But not the one she's entertaining. What she doesn't know is instead of joining Jesus in heaven, Jesus intends to meet Faith in the deepest, darkest hell she can imagine. For Jesus is waiting for her in the fractured depths of mental illness.

I Want to Die

Slumbering

Cats slumber the day away. So do I.
But what compels me?
At night I cannot find the threshold of rest.
My body tells me "You are ill!"
I scream. I cry. I die inside.
You cannot take my spirit away!

Then a soft knocking at the door.
Reality sweeps in
haughty, proud, undisputed.
With one piercing look
her message is quite clear.
I hang my head and weep.
She rocks in the chair until sunrise
Leaning her head back
with a contented sigh.

I tread dismal waters in search of sanity.
Wanting answers to questions
I'm clueless how to ask.
Where is the one I used to be
Who faced with grace and dignity
Tasks expected of me each day?
Where has she gone?
Perhaps she is dead.

She runs far, far away from me.
Why did she not take me along?
In horror and disgust,
I simply could not measure up.
Oblivion and defeat sleep with me.
Discouragement is my watchdog.

Have mercy on me, O LORD, for I am weak;
O LORD, heal me, for my bones are troubled.
My soul also is greatly troubled;
But You, O LORD—how long?
Return, O LORD, deliver me!
Oh, save me for Your mercies' sake!
For in death there is no remembrance of You;
In the grave who will give You thanks?
I am weary with my groaning;
All night I make my bed swim;
I drench my couch with my tears.
My eye wastes away because of grief;
It grows old because of all my enemies.

Psalm 6: 2-7 (NKJV)

1988

I wanna die.
To end the pain in my mind and spirit.
Depression seeps into my brain, blackening my every thought.
My body is oppressed with fatigue, lethargy, and apathy toward all but this infernal agony and grief.

I want to be alone.
Friends don't understand me.
I don't understand myself.

I am lost.
I am of no value to anyone.

Darkness descends as a familiar friend–justifying sleep. A soothing balm from the screaming inside–if only temporarily. My emotions are unstable–unpredictable. Wailing heavily, it seems as though a dam has burst inside of me. I feel as though my tears will never dry. Caught in a vise of helpless despair, I reach and stumble for anyone or anything to ease my pain. What is wrong with me?

I suck at this thing called life. I know this because all the voices within me reverberate with condemnation. My parents and my mother-in-law frequently remind me of my failure as a daughter, wife, and mother. Try as I might, my actions continually confirm their accusations.

I let my family down.
I let myself down.
I let God down, down, spiraling down.

Depression is a dragon wrapping its long serpentine tail around my neck suffocating me, digging its sharp nasty talons deep within my worthless soul. I can no longer bear the oppression of obligations, unfulfilled expectations, and the guilt and shame of constant failure. I long for rest. Sweet blissful eternal slumber.

Gonna die. Not anything painful, mind you. No knives, no ropes, but I must escape my meaningless existence. Steve and Josh would be better off without me.

Pills. Do I have enough pills in the house to take care of it? Yes! I think so! At least I can take a stab at it–no pun intended. But what to do with Josh? He's only four. I can't let him find his mommy dead.

Steve knows I'm depressed and all screwed up yet he doesn't understand.

"Steve, will you call someone to babysit for tomorrow? I'm feeling so bad, pleeease?"

"It's ten-thirty! Who could I call at this hour of the night? That's asking too much, Faith. Just go to bed and get some rest, you'll feel better in the morning."

I beg. No-argue. He doesn't budge. Defeated, I retreat to bed. Steve buries himself in a hotdog devoured by a fan on the second row of a televised ball game. God, I hate sports! I'm so mad I could spit!

I can't sleep. Reaching behind a small row of books on my side of the bed I pull out a Hershey's white chocolate with almonds candy bar. My private stash. The crunchy addition to creamy goodness tantalizes my taste buds but doesn't satisfy. I'm not feeling my usual sugar rush. Try as I might, candy can't fill the emptiness in my soul. I devour sweet white chocolate while dark thoughts consume me as I devise a bitter plan to end my life.

It helps-almost cheers me-to have a plan of action. I'll find a sitter for Josh. Then I'll take every pill in the house. There's plenty to do the trick. I don't ever want to wake up. I'll take all the pills, just to be sure. It's a good plan, but first...

Dear Steve and Josh,

I love you both very dearly-but I cannot go on. You deserve a better wife, Steve. Josh deserves a better mother.

I hope in time you will come to love another-to find the kind of mate you deserve. Remember I love you both very much. I just can't live with this pain any longer. Please forgive me.

Love,
Faith.

God, help Steve and Josh. Love them for me. Grace them with comfort. God, forgive me. I want to come to see You, but I don't know how You feel about suicide.

"WHAT HAVE YOU DONE?" Steve shouts, ripping covers off me in the middle of the night.

Jolted awake, I look at him in a stupor. "Why did you wake me up? You know I have trouble sleeping." Anger, hot and razor-sharp rages through me. "What's wrong with you? What time is it?"

Steve thrusts my note at me–found too soon. Oh, God! "WHAT HAVE YOU DONE?"

"Nothing. I was going to do it tomorrow." I attempt to rub the grogginess from my heavy eyes.

Steve sits on the side of the bed–tears streaming down his face. "I don't know what to do. I wish I could help you feel better. I need you. Josh needs you. Please don't do this, Faith."

The next morning I watch Steve back out of the driveway. Off to work he goes. Mr. Responsibility. Never misses work for anything. Don't you know how much I need you today? Can't you understand anything at all? I soothe my pain with a large pack of peanut butter cups before breakfast and an Eskimo bar after.

Our pastor has been talking to me for about a month. Depression only increases. Steve has arranged for me to see him again and has secured a sitter for Josh. I promised I'd keep my appointment. Steve wants me to show Pastor the note.

"This is totally out of my league," Pastor confesses. "I'm sending you to a doctor. There are new medications that work miracles for depression." I need miracles.

I also need a snack.

Driving to the doctor's office is a hoot. A large bag of M&Ms spurs me on.
Another stop sign.
Where am I? How did I get here?
I'm disorientated. Confused.
I'm fearful. Like a lost child in a shopping mall on Christmas Eve.
Angels must have guided me on the thirty-mile drive to the doctor's office.

A doctor prays with me. Mascara-mingled tears streak my face, sliming my makeup. Everything is surreal. Dreamlike. The room darkens in a swirling pewter fog. Maybe I'll wake up soon.

"Have you ever heard of a program called Rapha?" the doctor asks.

"No."

"It's a Christian treatment center I think will be beneficial to you. We're checking now to see if there's an available room for you."

Hospital? I just want to go home and sleep.
I can't make decisions on my own.
My mind has become eerily silent.
I'm shutting down, like the rusty Tin Man of Oz.

I'm on autopilot, doing what I'm told.
They're only trying to help. They care. I suppose.

Alone again, driving to the Rapha administration offices. God, how I wish I had someone with me. Stopping at a convenience store, I buy three candy bars and a bag of Corn Nuts to munch on the way. The Corn Nuts are salty like my tears.

Sitting at Rapha Administration Offices–waiting–waiting–waiting. I ache to lie down and sleep. What a mess. My bloodshot eyes are puffy–my face is blotchy from crying. Why did I come here? I just want to go home and sleep. Forever.

I'm ashamed of the state I'm in. I want to run and hide–like the massive run in my pantyhose snaking down my leg, burying itself in my shoe. Let me shrink to the size of a pea and roll out of here!

Slogging in a fog–exhaustion drags me down. Waiting feels eternal as a young lady answers phones and waltzes back and forth in the office. Oh God, don't let me be assigned to her. She has no professional demeanor at all. She's wearing flip-flops, for crying out loud. Who is she? Please, please, please, don't let it be her.

At last, she calls my name and ushers me into an office. Dr. Kathy, a well-dressed pretty brunette greets me. Thank God it's not Miss Unprofessional.

Dr. Kathy looks at me with interest. "What plans do you have to commit suicide?" Finally, someone believes me.

"Pills." She hands me a tissue for my tears.

"Will you do some play-acting for me? Pretend to be your mom and Faith just committed suicide. What will you say?"

I start crying again. "Faith, how could you do this to us? What will people think? What about all our friends and the members of our church? What about your father's ministry? You have ruined that forever. Everyone is going to think I was a failure as a mother because you committed suicide!" I look down and slowly shake my head. "Oh, Faith, Faith, Faith..."

This is an astonishing epiphany! Until now, I was not aware of feeling my daddy's position as a preacher was of greater importance to my mother than I was.

Miss Unprofessional interrupts our session. Dr. Kathy steps out of the room for a moment. Upon returning, she informs me there are no inpatient beds available.

"There is room for you as an outpatient until an opening occurs. I want to make a twenty-four-hour contract with you stating that you won't harm yourself." I sign the contract, feeling numb and clueless about being able to keep my word.

I'm admitted to the Rapha Day Hospital for eight hours a day to return home in the evening five days a week. Outpatient day hospital feels like adult daycare. Days drag on. I shuffle in a group back and forth from room to room where therapists lead various group sessions. Therapists here seem so young. Can they actually know what they're doing?

The week before being admitted to Rapha I tried to soothe my depression with sex with Steve. It always left me feeling unfulfilled, as though my needs were still unmet. I've always taken great pride in being a virgin when we married. Could it be possible I wasn't?

Therapists tell me I show symptoms of one who may have experienced childhood sexual abuse. I don't recall anything of the sort, but I want to know one way or the other if I'm suppressing some terrible memory of abuse. I muster the courage to face it. I want to be free. So in addition to other groups, including Addictions for an eating disorder, I join a Sexual Abuse Support Group.

On the way home each day I stop and buy candy, snacks, and diet Pepsi or Mountain Dew. The more intense the session, the bigger my purchase. What isn't eaten by the time I get home I hide in the car glove box. Or behind books in the bedroom...and den. Or behind unused cooking appliances in the kitchen cupboard. Oh! And inside my piano bench. That's a great place since I'm the only one in my family who plays the piano.

Food is my salvation–my comfort, my stress relief. It's my motivation, my reward for suffering through unpleasant experiences. Like group therapy. Sugar and salt are my drugs of choice–usually providing an appealing high. Too bad it's so very short-lived. And fattening.

Steve also has a sweet tooth. We indulge together. Still, I often eat in private because I don't want to share. And because I don't want anyone to know how out of control this has become. Who can say which is the greater motive?

Rapha

Madness

Madness.
Causing my mind to be crazy, gone, lost.
Sadness.
This disease binds me unmercifully.
Hopeless.
Uncertainty groping through time, searching for me.
Will I ever be free?
Grasping.
Holding to One unseen begging desperately.
Hear me, please hear me.
Screaming.
Cry, deny friends who betray.
Nothingness.
Empty, gone, all effort vain.
Purpose.
Unchanged. Relentless.
Bankrupt resources.
God alone decides.

> How long, LORD? Will You forget me forever?
> How long will You hide Your face from me?
> How long am I to feel anxious in my soul,
>   With grief in my heart all the day?
> How long will my enemy be exalted over me?
>
> Consider and answer me, O LORD my God;
> Enlighten my eyes, or I will sleep the sleep of death,
> And my enemy will say, "I have overcome him,"
> And my adversaries will rejoice when I am shaken.
>
> Psalm 13:1-4 (NASB)

1988

After five days of Rapha Outpatient, Steve escorts me to Rapha's Inpatient Unit. Massive heavy metal doors shut and lock like a tomb. Trudging down a seemingly endless hallway we finally come to the nurse's station. All my personal items are confiscated and deposited into a plastic basket.

The hallway echoes with horrific screaming and yelling from a nearby patient. I'm scared to get locked in this strange place. What's awaiting me? Will I be safe? I'm numb, like fingers playing too long in the snow. I want to run, but my body is frozen to the floor. This is voluntary, right? I'm ready to go home now.

I shuffle along, barely conscious of my surroundings. Steve and I are given a tour of the ward and shown my room. Two twin beds–two small chests, yet, I have the room to myself. What a relief. Still, I want out of here! The walls are closing in–terrifying me.

Visiting hours are over. "Please don't leave me, Steve!" I clutch his arm and cling tightly.

"I'll return tomorrow, I promise." Never one to disobey the rules.

Is there anyone in my life who hasn't abandoned me? Raised in a military town, friends came and went, yet I remained. Left behind. Abandoned. I hate telling friends goodbye over and over. I hate being left behind.

"What significant events have happened to you lately?" asks the smiling director.

"Well, my best friend just moved to Japan. We grew up together wanting to be missionaries. She's the only one of us fulfilling that dream. A dear friend I loved as a father died. I almost killed my son and myself in a car wreck. And I turned thirty with very little to show for it. Other than that, nothing much."

Questions, questions, questions. Mr. Smile's infuriating interrogation continues. All he lacks is a butt hanging from his lip and a spotlight to complete his third degree. Is there no end to these infernal questions?

He keeps smiling at me. I hate that! I'm here to be treated for depression and he's grinning like a dang chimpanzee! He may be trying to show compassion, but it drives me crazy! STOP SMILING!

Inquisition finally complete, I lie on my bed and stare out the window. Windows-not for opening. Thick double-paned glass with criss-crossed wire veins. No escape. Hopelessly, I draw the curtains on the world.

A sharp rap on my door and a witch in a white hat enters. "Your dinner is ready. Come and eat."

"Don't they bring food to our rooms?"

"No. If you're hungry you must go to the dining hall." Ludicrous.

Hot angry tears spill onto my plate while I eat in the cafeteria. Wretched tears! I can't stop them. I had hoped this would be a reprieve from my fishbowl, but I now find myself in a big tank. Everyone is staring. Go away-quit looking at me!

The next day I'm assigned to a doctor with a heavy Middle Eastern accent. He prescribes medication for anxiety and depression. He's here purely for the meds-no therapy. The first two weeks pass in a haze until meds kick in and I gradually become more coherent.

Depression. Pursuing me all my life. Showing up at the most inopportune moments-sucking the life out of me. Toying with my sanity-declaring war on my mind. Sometimes I resist. Usually, I daydream it away. Today my tormenting foe has me fully defeated.

My thirtieth birthday. I leave strict orders: No Party! No Cake! This birthday will be ignored at all costs!

You're thirty years old, girl. What's going on? Thirty years is supposed to be all grown up. Got it together time. But look at you. Always tardy. Never dependable. You still overeat. Your rear end is as wide as the length of five ax handles, for Pete's sake! Your son is precious. You have a loving and devoted husband. What more could you want?

You shouldn't be depressed. That's not the way Christians feel. If you really know God, you wouldn't be depressed.

My parents' phantoms are my demons. A constant cacophony of accusations reverberates through my head. I try not to think too much about them. They're just thoughts. It's normal. They're getting louder, though. The way a low rumble of a distant train crescendos until its thundering roar rattles my teeth.

God, *do* I know You?
God, where are You?
What does it matter?
I want to be left alone to die.

Monday I'm assigned a new therapist–a guy–Eric. I was comfortable as an outpatient with Dr. Kathy. I don't want to start over with a new therapist, especially a man, but there are no options. He probably won't understand premenstrual symptoms.

Come to find out, his wife suffers from PMS. So what do I know?

Some group sessions are for those who have chemical addictions. Others are depressed. They all make me nervous. I'm feeling fidgety and tense. Anxiety is unbearable.

"Who are you?" Eric asks.

"I'm Faith Alison."

"Yes, but who is Faith Alison?"

"I'm Steve's wife." His eyes ask for more. "I'm Josh's mom. I'm a children's choir director. I'm..."

"That's what you do. Who are you?"

Bewildered, I bite my lip. I furrow my brows in concentration. Who *am* I? I look up at Eric. "I don't know."

After much discussion Eric asks, "Aren't you angry?"

"Naw," I shrug, "I just have PMS."

"Depression is often anger turned inward. Couldn't you be angry at your dad for not letting you be an individual–not letting you express yourself? Could you be angry at God for taking away someone dear to you?"

Hmmm. I suffer from PMS and stress–but anger? Where is this guy coming from?

It turns out, Eric is a great therapist. We talk each day. He introduces me to the truths of God's word. His insight into how it applies to me is a type of understanding and teaching I've hungered for all my life. The wisdom Eric imparts is personal, practical, and Scriptural.

"You know, Faith, Jesus never commanded His disciples to follow Him. He just said 'Come and follow Me.' It was their choice. You too, must choose to walk your own walk with God–to have your own personal relationship with Him."

What does he mean? I try to follow God's commands. I try to do all the "Dos": I go to church, tithe when Steve and I can afford to, serve when I can, be a good person, et cetera. I generally don't do any of the "Don'ts": I don't smoke, don't drink, don't swear (often), don't dance, or wear pants (in public, that is).

"Never swallow anything without chewing it up first. Don't take anyone's teaching on God or spiritual matters as gospel. No matter who it is or how much you trust them. Always pray about it and ask God to show you the truth. Search the Scriptures for yourself. Then step out in faith in what you've learned."

That's a tough one. I'm not a Bible scholar. How can I know if something is from God or if I'm interpreting Scripture right?

"Until a person comes to the end of himself and turns to Jesus Christ, there is no healing. Without healing, there's only the reorganizing of the problem to achieve temporary relief. God makes us trophies of His grace by blessing us and then by receiving glory for our healed and redeemed lives."

How much more "end of myself" is there than wanting to die? Unless, of course, to succeed in doing so. Add that to my long list of failures.

"All error begins with truth. Truth starts with God. Satan perverts truth by using God's word out of context to deceive. He also convinces us of lies about ourselves based on circumstances or the way others act toward us."

I'm overweight. That's a fact. I know I'm not good enough at anything no matter how hard I try. I'm sure God is as displeased with me as I am with myself. He has to be! Voices in my head verify it often enough.

"Healing comes from learning how to identify lies and accept and act on the truth of God's word. Let God do the changing. He's the One who does the work in you. His works of grace are inside your heart, your spirit, and your beliefs."

Lord, I believe. Help my unbelief.

Like me, Eric is a musician. That can't be a mere coincidence. He plays the dulcimer, harmonica, and guitar–just to name a few. I wish he had his dulcimer here to play for me. He gave me a recording of his music, which I play every day.

Eric appreciates what music means to me. He encourages me to sing or listen to worship music in my room during my quiet time. Music links me to my new friend.

A brand new piano arrives on the ward! I can't believe it! This instrument is so new, it's never even been played! A steady flow of people passes by, yet, the piano is seldom played–ignored like a wallflower at a prom. I wish I could blink everyone out of the room.

The blond wood is sensuously cool to the touch. Ivory keys, smooth as cream. Surely Jesus provided this beautiful instrument to entice me to play and sing to Him. The piano beckons, "Come. Play." I need music for my spirit. I sneak into the break room early in the morning with the door closed and softly play. It provides a calming balm to my soul.

My body stiffens as someone enters the room. Several staff members barge in with songbooks and attempt to sing along. Trembling, I'm drenched in a cold sweat. I CAN'T DO

THIS! A lifetime of performing and people-pleasing, I can't do it here and now. The carnival spectacle–never achieving perfection. Insecurity crushes me like an avalanche! Hell in its purest form!

Shaking and crying, I run to my room. I cower in my bed, pulling the covers over my head, and try to sleep off the depression overshadowing me. The mask of performance is falling.

How can the past affect the present? Especially for a believer in Jesus? I've been a Christian since I was twelve. Why am I having such a hard time finding joy in life, or holding on to it whenever I find it?

To be honest, I thought giving my life to Jesus would solve all my problems. Being born again means my sins were washed away. Weren't issues related to those sins also washed away? The past is the past. It's over and done with. I should simply "build a bridge and get over it," right? I'm all for that! Sign me up!

Oh, wait! I need materials. I need tools. I've never built a bridge before. I need instructions. And I'm pretty sure I'll need some experience to build a bridge safe enough to cross. That means I'll also need an instructor.

That's where Rapha comes in. Rapha uses Robert McGee's *The Search for Significance* book and study guide. Through it, I learn to identify the lies I believe about myself and replace them with the truth of God's Word.

It's possible to live with scars from accidents or surgery without lasting mental anguish. However, early childhood abuse, neglect, inconsistent treatment, or harsh words can have lasting effects. Why? Because it instills messages that cause the individual to question their worth. And boy, do I question mine!

Common lies come in the form of performance, approval, blame, and shame. I believe them all, though not always conscientiously. I loathe myself when I fail to meet certain standards or lack the approval of others. I feel unworthy of love and deserve punishment when I fail. I feel incapable of changing myself.

Then there are triggers. Triggers are whatever compels me to overreact to certain situations. Lots of things can trigger reactions both pleasant and unpleasant. I overreact when my false beliefs feel confirmed by someone's criticism and judgment. It's worse when it comes from people I love.

I'm learning about something referred to as "Trip In." It's designed to help identify triggers when they occur. Asking myself specific questions and following a process should help me deflect triggers.

I'm supposed to try to identify the emotion behind the trigger. This is easier said than done as I'm often confused about my feelings. I'm to ask myself what my immediate reaction was and identify the false belief. This should enable me to reject the lies and replace them with the truth of who I am in Christ. Then I'm to believe in faith by accepting and responding to the truth. I can do all things through Christ who strengthens me, right? That's what I'm told.

Through the study, I'm beginning to see the truth–a mere glimmer of who I am as a child of God. I grew up hearing most of the scriptures we're studying. Why didn't they mean anything to me before now?

My sin separates me from God. The penalty for sin is death but Jesus took my punishment so I could be reconciled to Him. That means I don't have to fear punishment or rejection. Jesus gives me great worth apart from my performance so I don't have to fear failure. I've been made brand new, complete in Christ. That frees me from the pain of shame. I'm deeply loved, fully pleasing, totally forgiven, accepted, and complete in Christ.

This is not Daddy's hellfire and brimstone–just a quiet voice conveying what God had done for me. Better still, what it means on a personal level. Oh, if only I could fully accept it! The head acknowledges and accepts; the heart is struggling. It's so hard for years of habitual thoughts and feelings to agree with the facts.

My spirit quickens as a glimmer of truth warms my heart but it's subtly clouded by Daddy's perverted message–void of grace. The more I learn, the more I discover serious issues with my dad. This is a revelation. Fear of him and his opinion of me is stifling.

Sunday night worship is also refreshingly new. We sing and receive a message, but neither is like anything I heard growing up.

Mac, the therapist for chemical dependency, leads worship on Sunday nights. He uses cassette recordings from church services to introduce praise and worship. The songs are beautiful. I don't know any of them.

For that matter, I've never before heard terms like "praise and worship" or "singing praise to the Lord." In the church where Daddy preached and the Baptist church Steve and I attend, we always sing from a hymnal. We sing the same old hymns people have sung for several generations. I've sung them over and over almost every Sunday of my life.

Until now.

Whenever Mac doesn't have a tape, a group member, Darlene, leads worship. She's a professional gospel singer with an angelic voice. I admire her talent and ability to use her gift without fear or reservation.

I was at first intimidated by Darlene, but she drew me in, proving herself to be a caring friend. We sing praises to Jesus while I play piano. My confidence has bloomed under her encouragement and nonjudgmental support. Tonight we'll record background music on her expensive tape player. She's getting discharged tomorrow. I hate to see her go.

Eric leads tonight's service. He begins talking about how Jesus suffered the same pain everyone experienced. Even those of us in group.

"Jesus can relate to our suffering. He knows the depth of our pain. Scripture tells us, 'He was despised and forsaken of men, A man of sorrows and acquainted with grief'"

He reads C. Truman Davis' article, "The Crucifixion of Jesus: The Passion of Christ from a Medical Point of View." It describes in detail the severity of deep lacerations and flesh removal from broken pottery and sharp metal tied to the ends of several cords used for flogging, injury from nails piercing Jesus' wrists and feet, and how Jesus had to push His lacerated back up against the rough wooden cross to a standing position to keep from suffocating before finally succumbing to death.

"In His darkest hour, He experienced rejection and abandonment from those He loved. While on the cross, Jesus asked His Father why He had forsaken Him. He can relate to your suffering. He knows your heart. He feels your pain. He loves you and He cares. Best of all, He can and will heal you if you let Him."

My tears flow as Eric speaks. A sliver of light begins to penetrate my heart. It feels like I'm hearing the truth of the cross for the very first time. In all my thirty years of church attendance, I've never once felt the immense depth of Jesus' suffering like this. What Jesus did for me is amazing! Revelation of Jesus' detailed death on the cross penetrates my soul. It envelopes me—completely consumes me. It becomes so very precious I seek out songs about the cross to sing in quiet times at the piano.

I see Jesus in Eric's eyes, in his quiet soothing voice, in his communication with me. Sessions led by this man take on greater depth and meaning.

"Just a reminder, my twenty-eight-day training program ends in five days," Eric announces one fateful morning.

What? No! How did I miss this? My heart feels like I've been shoved down an elevator shaft from the tenth floor. Then the elevator crushes me. I can't do anything but sit and cry.

"It's okay," Eric consoles. "Grief is natural."

DON'T LEAVE ME!

Today is the day that Eric leaves. His training period is over, but my treatment is not. My four-week inpatient admission has been extended another four weeks. I want to beg Eric to stay.

An infinite loop of nightmares of abandonment has tormented me every night this week. I'm going to be abandoned again! Surely my distraught heart will explode. Speechless, I can't even cry. A massive lump threatens to choke me. I've finally met someone who could reach into my misery to help me sort through it and now he's leaving!

Dear Eric,

How will I know the butterfly is born anew without you prodding at the cocoon?

In heaven perhaps Jesus will let you play the dulcimer for all eternity. Thank you for the wonderfully refreshing touch your music-a gift of God-has had on my heartstrings. I equate it with David playing for Saul because I, too, have many demons haunting me. Your music touches me to the very core of my being.

I don't want you to go. I'm like a child being wrenched away from someone who gave me that first taste of the food Jesus has for me.

Life is not fair.
I love you with Jesus' love,
Faith

Wanting one last session with Eric, I camp out in the hallway beside a room where he's talking to another patient. Minutes are ticking away. Surely he'll allow time for goodbyes.

I divert my anxieties by tending to plants on the ward. I tease a fellow patient by spraying plant fertilizer on his meticulous hair. He retaliates by assaulting me with lewd accusations and vulgar innuendos. I am mortified. I feel violated-DEFILED!

I'm hit with a tsunami of unleashed rage-manifesting itself in a deluge of tears. WRATH! Unlike any I've ever known consumes me! Every offense plagues me as I stomp to my room. I pound walls and doors with brute force. My primal screams reverberate through the walls and down the hall. Years and years of pent-up fury erupts with volcanic force.

SLAM! These doors are slam-resistance. Ha! There's a first time for everything.
SLAM! I pour out unbridled vengence upon my door.
SLAM! Every wound I've ever experienced is afflicted.
SLAM! Every speck of humiliation and shame.

Four nurses restrain me to prevent me from harming myself. One of them suggests a sedative.

"I don't want a shot!" I scream hysterically.

They linger while I calm down. Nurse Peggy understands. I love Peggy. The Wicked Witch approaches with a breakfast tray. I want to throw the tray in her face but I'm restrained.

After a few tense moments, I decide if I calm down they may leave me alone. Taking a deep breath, I'm okay now. I am in control. Maybe I'll be able to leave my room, a civil human being. Maybe.

But then...

Perfect Hair knocks on my door. "Can I do anything to help?" After saying all those ugly things to me and he still thinks he's my friend?

"YOU!" Screaming, I chase him down the hall. "How DARE you speak to me AT ALL?!"

"I demand to talk to the director!" I may be depressed, or even a little crazy, but one thing I am is a lady! I don't deserve Perfect Hair's revolting remarks.

The director manages to stifle yet another yawn as I explain my situation. A lot he cares!

Eric has joined us. "Are you angry because I'm leaving today? Is that why you acted out this morning?"

"I am angry that you're leaving, but I'm not angry at you. It's not your fault. However, what Rick said to me was a different story altogether. I'm furious at Rick."

"You must confront him with your anger." Non-negotiable.

"NO WAY!"

I accost Mac in the hallway. "I have only three minutes to spare, Faith, so in short, you need to come to group and talk to Rick in front yof everyone." Mac walks away, leaving me in a quandary.

HELP! I can't do it! I shudder to think of it! I feel nauseous! I run to my room and throw myself on my bed. A deluge of hot tears soaks my pillow as my heart cries out to God.

Lord, I don't want to do this. I CAN'T do this. I can't confront Rick on my own. His words hurt too deeply. I have never heard words like those that came out of his mouth! Now they're saying I need to confront him. Please, God, deliver me!

I continue to pray quietly, seeking His face for several minutes. Finally, I envision Jesus walking beside a calm stream. He's coming to me. He is standing beside a huge tree, His arms beckoning. His Spirit sings to my heart. His music washes over me. A song for my soul. Visions of Jesus–water slowing the tide within me as a cool, clear pool. I receive strength from Him–strength to face my fear and confront my foe.

Dressed to impress–dress, hose, makeup–the works. I'll show Mr. Perfect Hair I'm a lady!

A knock at my door. "It's time to go."

I hate confrontation. I amble down the hall toward the group room where he is. I stop at the door and take a deep breath.

Mac starts the session. "Sit facing Rick so your knees are touching. Hold his hands to ensure there are no punches. Now, tell him how you felt when he made those remarks."

Touch him? Repulsion overwhelms me. Recoiling! NO WAY! GOD, HELP ME! My face grows hot and I begin to shake. Sweat runs down my sides. I want to run.

Rick takes my sweaty limp hands from my lap. I don't return his grasp. "What did I say that made you so angry?" All innocence.

"You talked as though you were in a guy's locker room instead of mixed company. What you said was extremely offensive. You said you heard me last night doing something obscene with my curling iron. That made me want to hang you from the weight machine and beat you to a bloody pulp!"

"I'm sorry. Will you forgive me?" That's too easy! You don't deserve it. My squinting eyes and tight frown shout refusal.

"Faith, you don't have to feel like it," Mac says. "Just decide to do it."

I say the words, but will I ever truly forgive him?

Anger breeds violence.
God compels forgiveness.
Maybe I won't live through this.
No such luck.

I stomp my way to the designated smoking area referred to as the Black Hole. I'm assaulted by a cloud of smoke and greeted by several occupants. I walk up to someone I know.

"Michelle, can I bum a cigarette off you?"

"I didn't think you smoked."

"I don't. Yet." She hands me a cigarette. I pinch it with my thumb and forefinger and lift it to my mouth as Michelle holds a flame to it. I fill my mouth with smoke as it lights up as I've seen others do. I inhale deeply and abruptly cough it out. My eyes water. My throat feels like it's full of dried leaves raked with a metal shrub rake and set on fire. I can't stop coughing.

Before I know it, I'm surrounded by smokers offering tips. "Take small puffs to start with. Slowly draw it in and blow it out. Breathe."

I'm not particularly interested in developing another addiction so I decide to fill my mouth with smoke and blow it out without inhaling. I don't get the "benefit" of nicotine (whatever that's supposed to be) but it gives me something to do as I calm down. It also appeases the rebellion roused in therapy. It's not as satisfying as candy but makes a more effective display. And it's not fattening.

Another vice I've adopted here is swearing. Therapists encouraged it as a means to release pent-up anger and constrict legalism. It's not intended as a permanent vice. The goal is to eventually replace suppressed feelings with healthy means of expression and resolution.

Dredging up painful memories has landed me in my room under a suicide watch more than once. I've been put in a padded room two times when there wasn't enough staff to watch me in my room. Not cool! Not cool at all!

I'm angry!

I'm angry at God, for arthritis, PMS, pain-mental and physical, and depression. I'm angry at myself for being depressed, for not measuring up, for not applying myself. Angry because I should be well enough to go home by now. I want to go home.

I'm angry at Rapha for adding stress to my marriage. This whole situation is putting way too much stress on Steve and me. For separating me from my son. I'm angry at Rapha for assigning Eric as my therapist, knowing full well he'd be leaving. For Eric leaving in the middle of my therapy. For not realizing sooner he was leaving and not having time for closure with him.

I'm angry at therapists for telling me to lighten up. For them encouraging me to express anger, to be rebellious, and then punishing me for doing these very things. I'm angry with them for giving me a deadline of this Friday to get it all together. I'm sure.

I'm angry at my mom for having expectations I could never live up to. For being so negative. For not being more supportive when I was emotional. For telling me to snap out of it. For being so talented yet having such low self-esteem.

I'm angry at my dad for acting perfect. For always being right. Always. For being in control. For not allowing me to express my feelings or opinions or make decisions. For being so tough whenever I was in physical pain. For being a workaholic. For being a preacher. For being manipulative. For always getting his way.

Eric was right, I *am* angry.

Confronting My Parents

♪ You Can Have It, Jesus ♪

You can have it, Oooh, Jesus, please take it.
I don't want it anymore–I give up.
The breaking point came long ago.
You're the only One to go to.

You can have it, Oooh, Jesus, Oooh.
I'm finally gonna give it up, Jesus.
You've been there all along
But I thought I was so strong.
Being superhuman is a futile game.
I should have called on the power of Your name.

You can have it, I give it up, Jesus, Jesus, Oooh.
You can have it, I give it up, Jesus, Jesus, Oooh.
You're all powerful and You know what is best.
I'll just trust You now, You gotta do the rest.
I can't do it anymore.

Nooo–I can't do it anymore without You.
You can have it all–my life, my ambitions.
Teach me how to trust and obey.
I don't want it anymore, Jesus!
You can have it. Please take it today!

> But You have seen,
> for You observe trouble and grief,
> To repay it by Your hand.
> The helpless commits himself to You;
> You are the helper of the fatherless.
>
> Psalm 10:14 (NKJV)

I don't trust this new therapist, Brian. He's too good-looking. "May I pray with you?" he asks.

"Okay." But I'm not a happy camper! I don't like starting all over again after being deserted!

"Lord, reveal to us what we need to know about the source of Faith's intense feelings and what You want to do for her today."

Suddenly, the room goes black! The electricity has gone off. I scream in terror. Blubbering, I frantically grope for the door. Just as suddenly, light returns and I am safe once again. I release a heavy sigh.

Brian asks, "When you were a little girl, did you need a night light to sleep because you were terrified of the dark?"

"Yes! How did you know?" I stare round-eyed with tightly clasped hands.

"The Holy Spirit just revealed it to me."

Gasp!

"Don't worry. God is a gentleman. He won't reveal anything you don't want me to know."

Mother is sick a lot. Maybe I made her sick because she almost died having me. She had a hysterectomy right after my brother was born. Then she had a nervous breakdown. My parents talk as though my brother and I are to blame. I feel responsible. She's not there for us physically or emotionally. She's too preoccupied with being a preacher's wife. She's a basket case about it. Her fears make life miserable for us.

Daddy travels a lot to preach for revivals. He's often gone for two or three weeks at a time. Mother says she lets us choose what we'd like to do when Daddy's gone. It doesn't seem so. I only know she screams all the time and slaps us at any moment for no apparent reason. I also remember the paddle she named Bad Boy. I try to stay out of arm's reach and to avoid Bad Boy as much as I can.

She says she's gonna get me a "black mama." That's okay with me if she's nicer than mine. Maybe I oughta run away and find me a black mama to love me. That'll teach her! I never know what to expect from my mother–a slap, a hug, or a blank stare.

I worship my daddy. He is pretty much my god. He's bigger than life to me, an extremely strong personality. He

way with people. They love him. Like flies drawn to a Venus flytrap, everyone is subject to his charisma. They come to sip nectar and SNAP! They're snared with no escape! Just like me.

Slick as a weasel, he's conniving and controlling. Guilt and condemnation are his rod and staff. His innocent flock is clueless. He lures the needy into his church and takes advantage of their ignorance. Daddy's regal attitude is much worse at home than in public. He expertly weaves control of our minds. Mother fears and obeys him, calling him "God's man." I wanna puke.

Family members, all masters of masquerade. We're enmeshed with each other. None of us knows where one person begins and another ends. We infringe upon each other's individuality.

Emotions are not allowed, especially anger. "Go to your room until you can get hold of yourself." They can't handle my emotions. Are all families this way?

I'm just a little girl who happens to be his daughter. He's the best! I hang around him, clinging to his trousers while he's greeting parishioners. Sometimes he tells me to let go. I'm jealous of the attention he gives to others. I need to get their attention too, so I shake hands, standing as close to Daddy as I possibly can.

I love Daddy and would do anything for him. Anything. I'm second place after his ministry. The ministry always comes first. A kettle drum pounds in my ears to the rhythm of my heart. He's not even looking at me. Don't cry. Not here. Not now. Whatever you do, don't cry in front of everyone!

nts me to shine for Jesus so I'm put on the plat-
̇-even though I'm very young. I sing okay. I'm
̇-getting lots of praise. Too much for such a

As a teenager, I play the piano. I sing. Practice. Practice. Practice. I must improve. There is no place for second best.

Sometimes Daddy takes me out of school to sing at weddings, funerals, or church services. I must be prepared at all times. My stomach is tied in knots. Sometimes he even asks me to sing a song right in the middle of a sermon! I feel vulnerable-exposed. Naked before the world. Always the princess. No one senses my humiliation!

"Did you see how obedient Faith was when I asked her to come up here? Some of you teenagers don't respect your parents enough to obey them." Daddy boasts. Daddy preaches.

Daddy said a bad word. I never heard him cuss before. I run screaming and crying and close myself in the bathroom. My idol has fallen.

"Faith, come out here." No! I need to be alone in my misery. My stomach is squeamish. Am I gonna be sick?

"It's the same as saying cow manure." His excuse. It's not the same anymore. Mother can say the same word, but she does it all the time. I knew she was fallible. But not him. I thought he was perfect. Not anymore. Daddy is no longer a god. Daddy is flawed.

Breaking away. I no longer need to live by Daddy's rigid rules and restrictions. I can decide for myself. I am, after all, twenty years old! Rebellion manifests itself in a simple pair of slacks. Daddy believes women should not wear slacks. I disagree.

Dare I risk Daddy's disapproval?
Risk God's disapproval?
Absolutely no! Not that!
The ultimate curse! Rejection from Daddy *and* God!
Slacks go. Dresses return.

I'm weak. I cannot resist Daddy's control.
Oh, if only I could! But how?

"You must confront your parents," Brian says.

WHAT? No-no-NO! If I see them I'll have an anxiety attack or pass out. Or both. Nope-not gonna happen! I grab the arms of my chair to keep from shaking. "I can't do that." The mere thought is terrifying!

"Fear of man is a trap. Fear of your father ensnares you. You must confront them, especially your father about controlling you. You must tell him you want the freedom to be your own person. Think about it. I'll be right here with you."

Another wall of fire I must walk through.

"Face fear. It's the most courageous thing you can ever do," Brian assures.

"But I'm not a courageous person!" I don't want to have courage.

"Courage is not the absence of fear. It's going on despite it. I'll be with you the entire time."

Finally, I fold. Brian arranges for my parents to come. Not for a visit, but a confrontation. God, help me.

Mother looks worried. Daddy sits glaring. Arms folded across his chest, his legs crossed, he's obviously on the defense before I even begin.

I stumble over the words. Writing them beforehand helps a little. The paper rattles in my shaking hands. I can't breathe. My parents are going to kill me. With a trembling voice, I manage to proclaim, "I want to be free. I need to be myself to make my own choices…" Brian helps me along, clarifying when needed.

Mother remains silent. Her round eyes shift back and forth between Daddy and me.

Daddy is fuming. "I won't be put on a guilt trip!" He must feel threatened. He attempts to intimidate Brian by boasting about his boxing days. Brian isn't impressed. Nor does he back down.

Wow! I've never seen anyone stand up to Daddy before! I'm actually safe with Brian on my side.

"I feel smothered by your rules and regulations." I'm finally having my say. Mother stares at me with a look of horror.

Daddy sets his jaw. "What do you mean?" I didn't really expect him to understand. I look at Brian with a plea for help on my face. He nods as though to say, "Go ahead."

"I am grown up now but still feel trapped by your beliefs, your approval, and your thoughts of me." Discussion continues and my parents leave.

I did it! I actually stood up to Daddy! What's more, I'm still alive! Thank God! Miracles do happen.

I was feeling pretty good about myself when I woke up this morning. That is until I hear Daddy's voice booming over the intercom. He's demanding to see me before taking the long trip home. I can't face him alone! I'm so scared I want to wet my pants! Daddy can't enter without someone releasing the lock from the nurse's station. Doors that once felt like prison bars have become sentinels.

"You don't have to see him," Brian assures me. "We can tell him you don't want to see him."

"No, I can't do that to him." Can't in more ways than one. Oh, but I desperately want to deny him access! Such an agonizing decision–to see him or not.

"I DEMAND TO SEE MY DAUGHTER! YOU CAN'T KEEP ME FROM SEEING MY OWN DAUGHTER!" His booming voice through the intercom can be heard all the way down the hall. Finally, I begrudgingly consent to see him if only to shut him up.

"What is this freedom you're talking about?" Daddy demands.

Looking him square in the eye I say, "I need freedom to be me."

"Is this because you want to dress differently? Are you sure you're a Christian? We need to get you away from here because I think you're being brainwashed." My heart breaks.

"Brainwashing" at Rapha says Christianity is not a religion. It's a relationship with God. The relationship is established through love, grace, truth, faith, and obedience.

Condemnation, guilt, shame, hopelessness, and fear are from Satan. Fear paralyzes and holds me captive to sin.

Religion binds me to people-pleasing and performance with rules, traditions, expectations, et cetera. It's madness. Literally. Sanity is more important than any form of man's success.

God's love is rain for thirsty souls. Love casts out fear of failure, judgment, and condemnation. By God's grace, the Holy Spirit convicts me of my sins and compels me to repent. This brings hope for liberty and eternal life.

Truth is the nutrient from which faith grows. Faith is essential for healing. Faith in God's ability to heal and faith in my ability to be healed.

Love and truth are worship in spirit because God is love. Seek worshippers who worship in spirit and truth. Seek balance in spirit and truth within me.

> Then you will know the truth and the truth will set you free. – John 8:32 (NIV)

Brainwashing? If so, let my mind be scrubbed and bleached clean of Daddy's religion.

Journal Entry

Trees outside the window gently wave in the morning breeze. Baby pines, like those in Colorado. I try to remember the scenery. I recall a hazy scene of pine-painted mountains.

Compelled to look up at the sky–wondering how to cry out to my Jesus for help–trying to ask Him to calm my nerves.

Then I see it–a shaft of light peeking through the clouds like a whisper of hope. For a few moments, I ponder–hoping maybe it's a sign. Maybe, like the sun peeking through the clouds, I, too, will burst forth to shine God's goodness.

Home

God Knows My Name

God knows my name and all about me.
He hears me when I call.
God knows my name, my every footstep.
He catches me when I fall.
He knows my every heartache.
He sees me at my worst.
God knows my name for He made me
Before I even knew He was.

Seeing then that we have a great High Priest
who has passed through the heavens,
Jesus the Son of God,
let us hold fast to our confession.

For we do not have a High Priest
who cannot sympathize with our weaknesses,
but was in all points tempted as we are,
yet without sin.

Let us therefore come boldly to the throne of grace,
that we may obtain mercy
and find grace to help in time of need.

Hebrews 4:14-16 (NKJV)

1988

I'm checking out of the hospital today waiting for Steve to pick me up. He'll have to help me pack three carts of stuff acquired in eight weeks. Including my electric typewriter! "Steve, will you bring me this? Steve, will you bring me that?" I had no idea how much there was until I had to pack.

I puff a cigarette as I sit in the Black Hole. Mac pops in to say goodbye. He grins, knowing this is my last smoke. I wonder if he's the one who sets out cigarette-related cancer warning pamphlets all around.

As much as I feared coming here, I'm gonna miss the close family ties we developed. I'll miss helping hands within reach–a ready ear–a hearty hug. So many people to lose at one time. I've lost a very special living arrangement. But then I knew I'd go home eventually.

The outpatient director warned me transition time would probably take around three months. Still, being so very lonely is surprising. I miss fellow patients, nurses, psychiatric techs, and therapists. Knowing I can't get up and walk down the hall to knock on Brian's office door leaves me hollow. I already miss him so much! It's hard to believe how much I resented this place when I first arrived.

Steve arrives and greets me with a quick kiss. He gives me a look I can't quite decipher. He roughly tosses my stuff into the car. He seems agitated.

"What?" I ask.

"Nothing."

"I'm sorry for all the junk."

"It's not a problem." I'm not convinced.

"Something's stuck in your craw. What is it?"

"You smell like cigarette smoke. Now the car reeks of it. Why, when smoking is only allowed in designated areas?"

"It is, but…" I focus on rubbing a finger back and forth over the door handle before sheepishly replying, "I kinda started smoking."

Steve's anger skyrockets shockingly fast and furious. "YOU WHAT? No, you didn't! Why on earth would you do something so stupid?"

"Well, there were two types of people in group. Some with chemical addictions and others were depressed. Depressed people just moped around and got nothing done. So I hung out with the addicts who were more energetic and productive."

"So you wanted to be cool like one of the gang!" Not a question, an accusation.

"No. Therapy got too intense one day and it freaked me out. So I went to the smoking room and decided to try smoking to see if it would calm me down—"

"So you're going to smoke cigarettes while I'm at work."

"No, I've chosen not to smoke anymore." I'm angry now. "However, I am tempted to buy a pack of cigarettes right now–but I've chosen not to."

"Will you really? Are you going to buy cigarettes?" Still raging.

"NO! I *said* I was tempted but CHOSE NOT TO!"

Steve continues shouting about the same thing. I tell him I don't want to discuss it anymore but he wants to rant and rave. He's not even listening. He's so unreasonable I'm not even going to bother telling him I didn't inhale. Ha! The joke's on him!

"Either stop talking about it or stop the car." That shut him up! Dead silence the rest of the way home is stifling, but it beats the alternative.

Right now, making Steve sleep on the couch is far more tempting than smoking ever was.

Journal Entry

Steve went to work yesterday, leaving me alone for the first time since getting out of the hospital. After all, he did miss a whole day of work. A noble sacrifice.

I'm awfully sad and lonely without my Rapha family close by. Missing the comfort of having people just a few steps away. There are some I miss more than others. I cry each morning–longing for them. I'm such a baby.

I tried calling several people but no one was available. Walked over to Diane's house too peeved to consider or even care how far it was. Visited for two or three hours. That was nice, but I still had a hard time–deeply missing everyone at Rapha. Made several calls from Diane's. No one was available–still! Once home I became lonely again. It was rough. Extremely rough.

Finally, Mac returned my call even though he couldn't talk long on his work phone. He suggested I go for a walk. The weather was nice so I went for a pleasant ten-minute walk. I finally stopped crying.

Talked to Brian last night. It felt strange talking on the phone. I prefer talking in person. Can't get eye contact over the phone. Still, I was very relieved to talk to him. I appreciate that he didn't cut me off.

We talked about natural grief and loneliness after living with so many people for two months. Brian mentioned patients in the hospital had also been sluggish recently. Possibly from saying goodbye.

Steve went ballistic AGAIN! This time because I walked to Diane's. Seems to me he's being paranoid and controlling. I told Brian about it. He advised me to communicate my needs to Steve. To ask him to pray with me and not try to fix or control me–to try to understand how I'm feeling.

Brian reminded me of how busy I was during my hospital stay. He said I needed to restructure my days at home–to write down what I needed to get accomplished. He asked about bringing Josh home early from my brother's house. I told him we had to wait until the weekend when Steve wasn't working.

Brian suggested spending time with the Lord in prayer and praise. He suggested staying busy and reaching out to friends, neighbors–whoever is available. I mentioned all the people I tried to call but couldn't reach. He said God is in control even in minor details, not just major ones. Perhaps God wants me to reach out to others not related to Rapha.

At least I'll be able to see everyone during the bi-weekly group meetings at the Rapha Center. Tonight is the first session. Maybe I'll get to see some of my friends. It'll be good to resume group and individual therapy with Dr. Kathy.

Talked to Steve for about four hours. Confronted him on his codependency issues. I'm beginning to worry about our marriage.

Journal Entry

Steve sat in on my session with Dr. Kathy as I shared my hospital experiences with her. She suggested I write it all down. Wish I had been more diligent about keeping a journal during the last two months. Told her about my day of rage at Perfect Hair. I told her about what happened during the group session and how the Lord showed Himself to me. I feel like I've been born anew.

Steve was bored. Dr. Kathy tried to help him get in touch with his feelings. As Steve tried to share, I reached out and took his hand.

"How do you feel about me taking your hand?" I asked.

"It feels like you care."

"I do care," I cried. "How can I get it across that I love you? How can I get you to see it's your choice whether you believe me or not?"

I'm worried about Steve. He mentioned being jealous of my therapy. I'm wondering if he's subconsciously trying to end up in the hospital. I asked Dr. Kathy if she thought Steve needed one-on-one therapy. She set up several marital sessions instead.

Singing to Jesus is the only way I can get through washing dishes. Steve came out of the bedroom saying he couldn't sleep because I was singing. I apologized and offered to sing quietly, but I needed to sing. He said he wasn't complaining. It felt like complaining to me.

Home from the hospital for only a month and already the stress is killing me. It sure hasn't taken long to get to me. I feel like such a failure. It's so depressing! Daily existence requires new survival skills I either haven't acquired or mastered. I'm not sure which. I wonder how much longer I can carry on this way.

Josh was jumping on the bed when I got in the shower. Screaming suddenly penetrates the sound of running water. Oh, no! That's serious!

Blood gushes from Josh's back, slashed by the metal latch on my neglected suitcase. My knees are weak! I don't think I can handle this. Wrapping him with gauze and a tee shirt, "It's okay, it's okay, Josh. Be still while Mama gets dressed." I throw dry clothes over my wet body. No time to dry my hair, it'll dry on the way. I scoop up Josh and rush him to the hospital.

Oh, why didn't I put that suitcase away a month ago?

You could have prevented this if you weren't so lazy!

Yes, Mother.

Thirteen stitches in my poor baby's side! I feel faint. Praise God for Jerry from church who has come for support. Seeing my extremely adverse reaction, he graciously steps in to console Josh during sutures. Nurses brace me outside the door. Josh's cries devastate me. I'm his mother, I should be with him, but my knees feel like jello.

This is all your fault!

I know, Mother. I feel guilty enough without your input.

Several stitches later the doctor inquires, "Did you do this? Have you ever beaten your son?" God forbid! I'm so unnerved! Do I look like I'm trying to hide something?

"No! I would never do such a thing! I told you, I was in the shower."

"I jumped off the bed and landed on the suitcase," Josh replies.

See, I told you she's guilty! She should have put that suitcase away long ago!

"I'm sorry we have to ask these things. You understand. Your son will be okay. You may take him home now."

But she's unfit! Surely she deserves to be punished!

During my next individual counseling session, Dr. Kathy notices how distraught I am. "Do you need to be readmitted to the hospital?"

"Go back?" Let everyone know how weak I am? "Never!"

"Do you want to try the day hospital again?"

"Whatever."

Back to five eight-hour days in Rapha outpatient. During group I confess, "I feel like life is a huge pile of crap I'm constantly having to wade through. Will it ever end?"

"There was a boy discovered fervently digging in a barn," says the therapist. "When asked what he was doing the boy replied, 'I figured with this much manure, there's got to be a pony in here somewhere.'" It feels so good to laugh for a change! Perception is everything.

The next day I arrive carrying a shovel. I'm wearing old gardening clothes and a floppy wide-brimmed hat. "Here I am, ready to dig up some crap!" I embrace their laughter.

"Oh, Faith! What a clever idea," someone laughs. "Let me anoint your head with oil for prayer. Here, I'll even anoint your shovel!" Odd, but whatever.

"Faith," the therapist announces, "I want you to work on relinquishing control. I don't want you to speak at all during group sessions for the next few days. You may choose to cooperate if you wish or not."

Man, that's crazy! My heart is pounding in my ears. "Piece of cake! I can handle it!" Humor masks dread. I'll use sign language or write notes. I'll show them!

Mike, who has never uttered a word before, is expressing painful feelings. I want him to know I care. I'm glad he's finally speaking up. I must let him know I identify with him. I want to reach out to him. I must speak. No one else is affirming him. I want to help him so much! Remaining silent is physical torture.

I grab the therapist's hand. I'm ignored.
My jaw is tightly clenched—my face is hot—my body tense.
I begin to squirm. I'm going to explode!
I've gotta get out of here. NOW!
I jump up and bolt.

I use the sitter's phone to make a tearful call to the therapist. She's relieved I am all right and asks if I'll return tomorrow. I don't know what I'll do for the next few minutes, let alone tomorrow.

I drive home erratically. If only Josh wasn't in the car I'd drive off a bridge and end it all. I won't go back. They're asking too much of me. I cry all the way home. Maybe I'll go back tomorrow, maybe I won't.

Journal Entry

I give up, Lord. Now the car is down. You know our finances better than me. We simply don't have $350 extra cash lying around to fix the car. Poor Myrtle, driving ninety miles a day did her in.

Lord, I feel as though You're letting me get knocked down once again just so I'll feel helpless and hopeless enough to trust You. Well, I do feel totally helpless this time, that's for sure. I desperately want to trust You. Things are looking right for a miracle just about now.

Please forgive me, God. I'm such an ungrateful wretch. You do have the power to take care of us and You know our needs better than we do. Please forgive me for not trusting You. Please forgive me for holding on to things instead of letting go and letting You take control. Total control, that is. Am I ever gonna learn to let You lead me–to let You have complete control of my life?

Lord, I'm so scared of losing our house and everything. Please forgive me. I know I should be willing to lose it all if that's Your plan for us. Everything we have belongs to You. You're the one who's given us what we have. Why can't I give them all up to You? Why can't I be completely willing for You to take or give or do whatever You choose to work out Your perfect will in my life?

God, it hurts to break away from my parents. As You know, I haven't heard from them since our confrontation. I'm not pleased with the strain in our relationship. How could I have grown up in a Christian home, only to be so completely enmeshed? I didn't realize who You were–or who I was–for that matter. It's all so confusing. God, I wish sometimes I had never heard the word codependency. Other times I'm grateful to learn and grow and for the chance to change.

With these compulsive behaviors, my daydream world is cracking up. I like the real world. In reality, my eating disorder scares me and I truly do want to have it all replaced with better life choices. To become a better person all around.

You know what I'm frustrated about? Constantly checking my every thought and word to see if I'm trying to control others. Am I manipulating to get my way? Am I trying to get attention or do I actually need someone to nurture me? Am I working on my issues as hard as I should be? Am I too dependent on this power, this person, or that one? Am I acting childish?

I have this incredible pain over recent losses. I really don't understand this. I spilled my guts to these people, forming special relationships. It's extremely painful to give up and yet, here I am, Lord, back at the day hospital like a stupid goose. Once again I'll have to face the terrible pain of saying goodbye.

What am I to learn from all of this? Will the pain never end? Or will I go on getting deeper into therapy and digging up more and more issues to deal with?

I'm a chronic complainer. Yep, that's me all right. How in the world do You put up with me the way I've been talking to You? I deserve a couple of slaps or something for being so disrespectful and rude. Dr. Kathy said You're big enough to handle my anger. I hope she's right, but I'm still not very comfortable expressing my anger to You, the ultimate authority.

Please change me, my heart, my attitude, my false beliefs, everything about me. I'm really a mess. God, won't You please help me—please heal me? Please cover me with Your love.

The little girl in this grown-up body wants somebody big enough to take her on his lap and hold her real tight. She wants him to love her till all the empty spots go away. Well,

God, You're the only one big enough to do that. This little girl doesn't fit on anyone's lap. I need You, Jesus. In Your name. Amen.

"I want to use guided imagery with you," suggests the counselor.

"I don't know about that, Shawn."

"I'd like to teach you a relaxation technique to help you open your mind to enable you to get in touch with your inner child."

"All right."

"I want you to look out the window at a cloud and picture Jesus coming down out of that cloud, walking down to meet you. Now, close your eyes and relax. Tell me what you see."

Nothing...No wait!

"I see Jesus coming to meet me! He's thirty-something, wearing beautiful, soft blue and purple robes. He's smiling at me, reaching out His hand. I see His scars. 'These scars are for you.' I take His hand and we walk down a very long hallway.

"'Do you want to meet God, the Father?' Clinging to Him, quivering, I take a deep breath and nod my head. He opens huge doors. Blinding light bursts forth as we step into the room. Clinging to Jesus, He whispers, 'It's okay, I will go with you.'

"I'm now a small girl around five years old approaching the throne of God. I peek from behind Jesus and look at

God the Father. His hair and clothes are radiant white. His eyes, piercing. Light permeates His entire being like a great beacon.

"He's taking my hand and leading me to an enormous throne. Turning, He's now the Father and is drawing me to His lap."

I stroke His beard–it's so soft! I have His undivided attention. He wears no watch. I am important to Him. Jesus won't abandon me. He has time just for me. Jesus loves me. Weeping, wrapping my arms around myself in a hug, I embrace Him. "He's singing to me. We're singing together. He's stroking my hair." I lean my head into His strokes. I never, ever want to leave His lap.

"You must come back up the hall," Shawn's voice directs.

"No. I don't want to leave God's lap."

"You may sit on His lap any time you like. You only need to ask."

I am with you always. God the Father sets me down and rises. The Father becomes Jesus once again, smiling, taking my hand, we head toward the hall. I smile.

"What's happening now?" Shawn asks.

"Jesus and I are dancing. Laughing, holding hands as we pass through the hall."

Overcome with pure joy, uncontrollable tears run down my face, leaving me weak and drained. In silent awe, I ponder over what just happened.

"Good morning, Dr. Logan."

"Good morning, Faith. You're very early today."

"I know. I was hoping to catch you before devotional. I'd like to read a passage that's been dear to me this week. It's Matthew 28:20 'And surely I am with you always, to the very end of the age.'" Tears roll down my cheeks as I share my recent experience.

As I'm reading, a secretary named Cheryl begins weeping. She jots something on a memo pad. "God has given me a word for Faith," she says as she hands the note to Dr. Logan.

He reads it aloud. "The boil has been lanced and the healing has begun." Really?! There's no way anyone could possibly know I had lanced a big blister on my foot this morning.

As Dr. Logan prays Cheryl and I cry, intensifying into abject sorrow. I'm deeply moved. It's as though she's reached so far within the depth of my heart, unbridled grief overflows from both of us. I feel like I'm looking in a mirror, except the face looking back isn't mine. The release is like we've drilled a well and hit a gusher. As she continues to cry, my internal pain diminishes. How can this be?

"Have you ever heard of intercessory prayer?" Dr. Logan asks. I shake my head. "The Holy Spirit is allowing Cheryl to feel your pain so He can perform surgery on you."

As Dr. Logan prays, I feel the power of God, unlike anything I've felt before. We pray and raise our hands to God. Cheryl sobs again.

"The Holy Spirit isn't finished yet." We continue praying.

"God wants to hold you on His lap, Faith." I cry in response. "Do you want to sit on my lap?"

I'm no small woman! "I don't want to crush you. I'll just kneel beside your chair and lay my head on your shoulder if that's okay."

Jesus is holding me, telling me how much He loves me. I reach up and touch his soft beard, which turns out to be Dr. Logan's white beard. He smiles.

"I asked the Lord, 'What if she wants to stay here forever?'" He chuckles. "I heard Him say," using an Israeli accent, 'So what if she does?'" The experience has Cheryl and me completely drained. I'm flabbergasted that such a thing could happen.

The next day I feel like a new person. Wearing a skirt, blouse, and hose, with shoulders back I confidently stride into the room. Approaching Dr. Logan, I firmly shake his hand,

"Hi, I'm Faith Alison, an awesome spirit being."

Letters

Preacher's Girl

Daddy was a preacher.
Mother was his wife.
Brother was the one who acted out the strife.
I just gave it all I had for most of my life.

We must please the people. We must please God.
Be sure to say "Yes, Ma'am" and give a little nod.
Listen to the preacher, sit up straight in the pew.
You must be very careful,
'cuz everyone's watching you.

Never be too angry, Never frown or fuss,
And most of all the preacher's girl
should never fret or cuss.
You reflect your daddy in everything you do.
So straighten up that face, girl,
they're all watching you.

Don't show too much emotion, don't ruin your song.
After all, young lady, don't forget where you belong
You are just a puppet on a giant stage,
Just sing and play the piano. See the people are amazed.

"I don't really know you. To me, you're just a song.
Don't give me any trouble. Just sing and play along.
You enjoy the music, so that's the string I'll pluck.
I'll play you right into my hands
and you won't kick or buck.

Don't show too much emotion, don't ruin the song.
After all, young lady, don't forget where you belong.
You are just a puppet on a giant stage,
Just sing and play the piano.
See, the people are amazed.

I will get the glory. I will get the praise.
Faith is so perfect. Junior's going through a phase.
When you are such a good girl I can say with ease,
That God up in heaven is mighty, mighty pleased."

Now don't you be unhappy, you have got it good.
Some would kill to take your place if they only could.
Daddy won't you listen, listen to me please?
I played your game for 30 years,
now I need some peace.

Daddy was the preacher.
Mother was the wife.
Brother was the rebel.
I was the sacrifice.

Hear, LORD, when I cry with my voice,
And be gracious to me and answer me.
When You said, "Seek My face," my heart said to You,
"I shall seek Your face, LORD."

Do not hide Your face from me,
Do not turn Your servant away in anger;
You have been my help;
Do not abandon me nor forsake me,
God of my salvation!
For my father and my mother have forsaken me,
But the LORD will take me up.

Psalm 27:7-10 (NASB)

Journal Entry

Dear God,

You seem so far away, yet somehow close.

I've been putting off writing this letter because I'm not comfortable with the anger I have toward You. My heavenly Father, please forgive me for being angry.

I'm not happy with the way things are going for us right now, especially financially. Lord, every day this week I've been praying for money to come one way or another. It's really hard to not worry when things seem to keep getting worse. Steve is too paralyzed by fear to look for a second job.

I feel so helpless. Where are You when we need You? I know that sounds rude and disrespectful, but it's how I feel. I'm so frustrated and angry.

We try to be responsible with the income You've given us, but we're still having to struggle. It doesn't seem fair. Lord, we've gone without clothes, recreation, new cars, and house improvements in order to maintain a reasonable standard of living without using credit. We're trying our best to become debt-free. And then this whole year happened.

Doctor and pharmacy bills are keeping us behind with no way to catch up. I'm grateful for the insurance coverage, Lord, and for the fact that we still have a house. But I'm filled with fear about what next year will bring. How are we going to make it?

I know all we have comes from You, Lord. We're supposed to trust You and depend on You for our needs. But I'm having a rough time turning loose of these worries and trusting You to take care of us. Can You lend me a hand here, Lord? I could use a little help with this trust issue. I want to have more faith and believe You have everything under control. Why don't I trust You more?

Thank You for all the things You're teaching me through the people You allow me to come into contact with. I appreciate that there's help available in the area we live in. I love the new friends You've brought into my life as a result of my stay at Rapha.

I resent the fact that I'm not healed by now. It's hard for me to accept. The fact that I may be in recovery until I see You face to face. The reality of having to face the same issues for the rest of my life doesn't sit well with me. It seems strange to me that my friends are getting a handle on things a lot quicker than I am. I should be all better, or at least ready to give life a chance, You know? Some of them have been through a lot worse than I have. Why can't I get well too?

Sincerely,
Faith

Unsent

Dear Dad,

I'm forcing myself to write this letter because I have to own what I'm feeling about our relationship. I don't want this seething rage to have control over me any longer.

I love you, Dad, but I'm also very angry with you. I wish I could feel only love for you or only hate. Instead, I have a mixture of the two and it's very confusing.

Why did you have to be so perfect in my young eyes? Why couldn't you let me see you fail or suffer or make normal mistakes? You were always so strong, never showing weakness when sick or in pain. I was emotionally weak and therefore distasteful to you.

The one time I heard you swear I felt like my world came crashing down. You tried to make light of it, but I cried and cried. My god had fallen off his pedestal. Yes, I worshiped you in a twisted idolatry that caused me to see you and God as essentially the same. I believe you deliberately fueled that misconception in word and deed. You told your family and parishioners to look to God as you manipulated guilt trips to get us to do "God's will" according to your interpretation. You think you're entirely right and the rest of the world is completely wrong.

My distorted view of God hindered my personal relationship with Him. Of course, you always said, "Keep your eyes on Jesus and not on me." But you know, a person has to know Jesus before they can keep their eyes on Him.

You were fun to be around. People liked listening to you spin yarns and tell of your military experiences. There was a charisma about you that seemed to draw people to you and you to them. You enjoyed the admiration and respect of others. And yes, you also enjoyed the attention you received as a pastor.

It seemed to me like the people you ministered to were more important to you than your family. You always dropped everything you were doing to rush off to help someone. When I was little you frequently traveled while preaching revival meetings. I missed you, Daddy.

I've always wanted your approval so badly, Daddy. I would almost bend over backward to get it from you. Now that I look back, I figure I was your little dog to show off to the world. "Look what Faith can do. She can sing," or when I was older, "Sing and play for Daddy."

Why in the world would a four-year-old have to perform for others? How could you do that to me? Don't you realize the performance complex it gave me? Oh yes, I enjoyed it because you were proud. I got a lot of praise from people-as long as you approved. I was in heaven because my whole world was wrapped up in pleasing you and others. Mostly you. I learned to expect attention, thinking I belonged in the limelight all the time.

I became so comfortable with all the attention, I developed ways to keep it in small or large groups. I practiced long and hard to sound my best. I memorized lyrics and practiced so my performance would be perfect. So others would applaud. You were so perfect, I had to be too, didn't I? I was, after all, my father's daughter.

You used me, Dad, to receive praise from men. Yes, God gave me musical talent and a love for music, but you used me for your purposes. I'm mad about that. Why couldn't you have let me have my own identity? I was nobody until they realized I was your daughter. Then, instant popularity, instant appreciation. Almost all the praise you gave me was just to manipulate me to perform some action you wanted.

You were too busy for your family for quality time. You prided yourself in taking us fishing or Junior hunting. But there were almost always other people along for you to joke and entertain a majority of the time.

Yes, we were close as a family–too close. So close we thought we had to move in sync with your wishes as a whole with no room for individuality.

Church services always came first before homework and extracurricular activities. And yet you expected me to make good grades no matter how much time I had spent at church. Developing my mind was insignificant compared to church functions.

I always loved learning at school, but your strict dress code made me feel like an oddball. My esteem was very low and I always felt like I stuck out like a sore thumb. I was extremely uncomfortable. I hated the unwelcome attention my weird pauper's clothes brought. I still resent not being allowed to take band because the girls wore pants to march in. I would have enjoyed the opportunity to learn to play an instrument other than the piano. I couldn't even participate in gym class because of uniform shorts. I might have learned to be active enough to burn off some fat.

What really hurts is I actually believed you wouldn't love me if I didn't do exactly as you wished. I still believe it. You won't accept me on my merit as a person. Not without conforming and complying with your standards and beliefs. Knowing my expression of emotion is not acceptable behavior to you. That my true feelings about issues are unimportant. Oh, I tell myself you'd still love me if I chose to do wrong, but deep down I wonder.

I love you so much it hurts. I'm learning I have a separate identity besides yours. I'm realizing my negative sense of self-worth came from you. But needing your approval is a false belief. Did you hear that? It's false, false, false. I don't need your approval to feel good about myself.

My Jesus accepts me, loves me, and forgives me. He is the only one I need to please. Nothing I can or can't do will change how He feels about me. I am completely pleasing to Him. Did you hear that, Dad? I don't have to perform anymore. He loves me. He created me. He thinks I'm pretty neat, just the way I am. He is in me and that's all I need. His Spirit within me, loving me, teaching me, holding me.

I guess you could say that in a sense I don't need you anymore, at least not in a sick way. I no longer have to meet up to your standards or perform for your or anyone else's approval. I can be free. I must love you as my earthly father. Not some demigod to worship. Just my dad whom I love dearly as an adult, not a little girl or baby.

I no longer have to lean on your faith in God. I'm learning to grow my faith and relationship with Jesus. I love you,

Daddy, and I know it wasn't all your fault. You did the best you could with the knowledge you had. I forgive you and pray that you will experience healing yourself from the touch of God's hand.

Sincerely,
Faith

Unsent

Dear Mother,

There's so much I've wanted to say to you for so long, I hardly know where to start.

That day when you and Dad came to Rapha so long ago, you were very quiet, almost like a frightened little bird. I thought you might be too fragile to go through any sessions we may have. I suspected you identified with me more than you were willing to admit.

Dad has always been first in your life. I now see how dependent you are on him. People say you and I are alike, and I have to admit they're right, even in our looks. I used to hate it whenever anyone said that, but not anymore.

You used to be so much fun, Mom. When Junior and I were little you would play with us. We ran around chasing each other through the house. We wrestled or tickled or squirted each other outside with the hose. We had a lot of fun times when you felt well. But you didn't feel well much of the time. I hated when you were sick.

There must have been a lot of pressure on you as the pastor's wife, resulting in your being ill so much of the time.

When you switched me on the legs, it felt like stickers were on the switches. I thought you enjoyed spanking us. I hated when you called me a little devil, although I probably acted like one.

When I was older you would tell me you hoped my kids were ten times meaner than I was. I felt hurt and angry. I somehow believed it would come true. Almost everything you said was going to happen did happen.

I hated when you screamed at us. And we never seemed to do anything right. I made a vow never to scream like that at my kids. Yet I do the very same thing now with Joshua.

I hate that you are always right. Boss, boss, boss. I wish you had never said to me, "No, you can't do this or that because you are the pastor's daughter. No, no, no. What will the members think? What if somebody sees you? How do you think it will look if...? You need to be an example for the other children. So and so thinks a lot of you so you should go to visit her, etc.

Even now you're too hung up over what the church people will say. You won't go shopping because someone might see you spending money. It's ridiculous, Mom. It's a terrible way to live, always looking over your shoulder to see who's watching your every move. I hated it then. I hate it now.

I hate the scrutiny placed on pastors' families by church members and the world at large. It feels like we're living in a fishbowl. We're to be wonderful specimens of humanity, never rude or unruly. Loving tones to even the wickedest witch who ever darkened the church door.

I hated when you claimed indifference over things you cared about to prevent dealing with it at the time. I hate when you put yourself down saying you weren't very smart when in actuality, you *are* smart. You're one of the most intelligent women I've ever known. Dropping out of high school doesn't make you stupid.

I could never quite measure up to your talents, yet you expected me to. You had a way of being able to do something after only one demonstration. It's no wonder you were frustrated with my endless questions. I had to be shown how to do something more than once. I felt so frustrated at not being like you.

I truly wanted to please you, Mom. I'd clean the house while you and Dad were out making visits or counseling with someone. You'd come home and say you wished I had done something else or I should have done it differently. You found something wrong with every meal I've ever cooked. Everything has to be done precisely the same way you do or it isn't good enough.

Sewing was never fun. I always had to rip out seams because they weren't perfect. Now I get very tense when I sew because it has to be perfect. I once told you when we get to heaven you'll probably remake all the angel robes because they wouldn't be perfect enough. I remember it hurt your feelings.

I feel like as I grew older I was kind of competing with you to be creative and talented. I know I was mean to you during my first year in college. When I said you didn't sing on key. You refused to sing for such a long time. I was terrible. Mom, I'm sorry.

Whenever I was emotional, which was often, you never had any patience with me. "Snap out of it. Handle it. You're never going to make it if you don't get yourself together." All I ever wanted was some time, love, and affection from my mother.

At times you seem to enjoy pointing out my flaws, sometimes in a joking manner, but it always hurts. You like to tell people how mean I was to Junior when he was a newborn. That always made me feel bad. Give me a break. I was only eleven months old when Junior was born. I was still a baby myself.

In a lot of ways, I felt responsible for your illnesses. You seemed to have had physical problems ever since I was born. You almost died when you had me. I felt somehow we were to blame for all your ailments. You said that's when all your problems started, when you had children. Fear of becoming ill if I had a child plagued me until I had Joshua. Even now, whenever I consider having another, I'm afraid I'll develop poor health like you.

I hated wearing replicas of your dresses. They looked like old ladies' clothes on me. I always wanted to wear pretty, soft feminine colors with ruffles and lace, but you said they'd make me look bigger. Only tiny petite little girls could wear them. You know what I heard when you said that? I heard "You're different. You can't ever look like other girls because you're fat."

Remember those awful braces I had to wear when I was three and four? Instead of helping me go to the bathroom when I woke up one night, you told me to go back to my room. I felt unacceptable to you like I was a burden and bother to you.

I always wanted you to make my wedding dress. I dreamed of the kind of beautiful creation you would sew for my wedding. But you were ill again and I had to wear an outdated borrowed dress and a veil that didn't look good on me. You told me later you didn't want to make my dress because you figured I would back out of getting married and all your work would be in vain. That really hurt!

I see you differently now, through sympathetic eyes. When young, I thought you were two-faced with a happy church face and an angry mother face.

I now see you as a very needy person who has used illness and depression in your search for love and nurturing. I love you, Mom, and I really wish you could be healed emotionally.

You have taught me many valuable things. Practical everyday things like cooking, cleaning, and caring for my husband. Being creative on a shoestring budget. I know now that you did the best you could with the knowledge you had.

I wish you could understand me and give me some affectionate mothering. I have a lot of bitterness in my heart because I didn't receive some very important nurturing from you.

I'll be working on forgiving you. I choose to forgive you. For neglecting my emotional needs and for the emotional abuse I received. I pray our relationship can one day be the healthy one that God wants us to have.

Your loving daughter,
Faith

Unsent

Dear Mother and Daddy,

Please find enclosed a tape of the services of Victory Baptist. I sang and gave my testimony on a Sunday night as the Lord led me. Jesus has shown me what He created me to do–that is to write songs for Him as He gives them to me. Praise His name. The two songs on the tape are songs He wrote through me. I haven't shared this with you before because you haven't been supportive of my songwriting efforts. This used to hurt me deeply. Now I really don't care if you like them. Jesus likes them and that's all that matters to me. Now, the way I look at it is they are His songs and He lets me share them with Him. He's chosen me to give these songs to the world and only He can work that out.

We plan to come for the celebration of your 35th year as pastor. I would love to sing some of the songs the Lord has given me and any other songs of His choosing. In the past, my singing has been to please you and to perform for the church. Now it's just between me and Jesus and it's a whole different ball game. There's one thing I need to mention. I no longer have the same standards of dress that you adhere to. No longer will I put on a front to appease you. I believe God is concerned with my inward walk with Him much more so than my outward appearance.

I also believe He is pleased with me and that I am in His perfect will for my life. I will come prepared to sing because I'd like to, this being your last anniversary and all. It will be between you and the Lord if you ask me to sing. What I sing will be totally up to Him.

This fall, I plan to return to school and obtain my music degree so that I can give a fully developed talent back to Jesus. It won't be easy, but it's for Him I'm doing it so I can't fail with Jesus behind me.

I'm thankful for the way music was a big part of our family when I was growing up. It helped to nurture the natural talent that God created in me from the start. Some of my fondest memories are of you and your friends singing around a campfire or gathering around the piano to sing hymns. That legacy will remain with me my whole life.

I'll be singing with friends wherever the Lord leads in the coming months. After you've had time to pray about it, perhaps you would also consider praying about them coming with me to sing.

Well, I've got to close now. Hope this letter finds you both well. I would like to have a report on what your eye doctor says about your eye, Daddy.

With love,
Faith

Note: Sent a tape of music with a brief offer to sing instead.

SENT with an enclosed Form of Agreement

Dear Mother and Daddy,

We're looking forward to visiting you next month! We'll probably camp at KOA places along the way. That's our plan. We'd like for your house to be a place our family can come to on vacation. There are some important things we need to agree upon for that to happen.

Our family has made many lifestyle changes we want you to be aware of before we arrive. One is that we all three wear shorts and jeans now. We'll be wearing them on our visit to you. Another change we've made is in our choice of churches. We enjoy the church we're current members of and don't plan to make any changes in that area of our lives.

What we want from you, Mom and Dad, is an agreement not to discuss these changes with us. Only if we choose to bring up the subject. We don't want our manner of dress or choice of denomination to be open for discussion at any time. Not during our conversations, prayers, or sermons when we're in attendance.

We especially don't want Joshua to be the focus of any criticism or persuasion during our visit. Joshua has a very updated hairstyle. It's not long, only different. You may or may not find it amusing. Please don't hurt his feelings by attacking his chosen style of haircut.

We accept that your beliefs are still the same as in the past. That is your chosen path. We hope someday you'll be able to accept our differences. We've made these choices from our personal growth and relationship with God.

Please reply to this letter by June 20th so we can make the necessary arrangements for lodging. If you choose to disagree, we'll accept it and make arrangements other than staying with you.

We miss you and want to see you. We've both been working extremely hard, putting in a lot of overtime hours, to be able to afford this trip. We want to have lots of fun while there. We deserve it!

Please use the attached form to respond to us as soon as possible. We've enclosed a stamped self-addressed envelope to simplify mailing.

We love you and can't wait 'til July!
Love,
Faith

Note: Did not receive a reply so we enjoyed a well-deserved trip to Montana instead.

From Steve

Sweetheart,

I'm taking a moment of busy work, haha, and writing a note to you. In my head, I can imagine elegant, eloquent, pure, refreshing things to say–words that melt off the page. But alas, here I sit with pen in hand and my mind is as blank as a door knob. But here goes.

I haven't said so lately, but you are a blessing to me in every way. You are a Godsend in my life. You add to what makes my life complete and fulfilled. We've come from one end of the spectrum to the other, and though battle scars are evident, we are still alive. We've persevered each moment to where we are, and have now moved up to the next level, if you know what I mean.

Without God to direct our way, I feel we'd be lost. Sometimes it feels as though God is directing everyone but us. You and others have tried to convince me that it isn't so.

I like your renewed determination and commitment to giving God your everything. The new songs God has given you seem to inspire your very being. Someone long ago said that the only way you'd be happy was to embrace music to its fullest. I have to agree. I now see God's creativity in your music. It is my hope your music will touch and encourage whoever hears it. Keep it up, honey. You were meant for music and music was meant for you.

I love you, honey. You are what I want and need in a wife, period! May God bless you and keep you strong. May He give you the peace you so long for.

Your loving husband,
Steve

Eating Disorder

Delicious Temptation

Treats beckon me, whispering,
"You need this. Just give in, no one will know."
Like a naughty child, it tells me I can eat it alone.
No one will care. It will be all right.
It tastes so good.
Smiling, deliciousness drips with temptation.
I do not resist.
For good or bad, I deserve it.
Just this one time.

But the one turns to many
and I am left with chocolate smeared on my face.
Like a toddler asked, "Did you eat that?"
She shakes her head no,
but the evidence is smeared across her face.

If it's in the house I hear it call to me,
"Come and eat."
Even when out of sight, I hear it mocking me.
Pulling me to indulge.
"Enjoy the reward, just this one time.
You can resist tomorrow, but tonight, give in."
"Please shut up!" I scream.
Yet, it's relentless.

So I eat and eat and eat some more.
Not until I'm sick, only satiated.
For now.
I won't indulge again.
See? I'm satisfied.
Until I hear the call again.

> "Oh, that my grief were fully weighed,
> And my calamity laid with it on the scales!
> Can flavorless food be eaten without salt?
> Or is there any taste in the white of an egg?
> My soul refuses to touch them;
> They are as loathsome food to me."
>
> Job 6:2,6,7 (NKJV)

1989

Weekly sessions in private therapy and various groups help me get by. I'm learning coping skills for stress and dealing with anger and depression. I work on establishing healthy boundaries and building personal relationships.

Writing exhaustive letters to offenders gives voice to my pain and anger whether I choose to send them or not. I've hurled unbridled fury at empty chairs where sit envisioned enemies and offenders. I nurture my deprived inner child. Psychological techniques designed for survival, never touching–least of all penetrating overwhelming agony resisting appeasement.

Facing haunting memories is nauseating. Morsels of insight here and there are barely enough to survive on. Head knowledge floating in the shallow region of my brain. Nowhere near tapping the depth of my soul where my anguish festers. Mere crumbs to a starving spirit.

Crumbs like the ones I found when Mother wouldn't let me eat because I was too fat.

I like food. That's all there is to it. I want to eat everything and anything. I like sweets. I love chocolate. My idea of heaven is rolling around in a dry Olympic-sized pool filled with M&Ms. I gorge on sweets when depressed. Or stressed. Or anxious. Or hurt. Or hungry. And sometimes in between, just because.

A woman at Rapha had an extreme eating disorder that was much worse than mine. She ate all the labeled leftovers we members put in the refrigerator. I figured she would eat my food so I put a sign on one of my bowls saying, "Eat this and you are dead meat!" She didn't eat it. But then, she wasn't there very long.

I can't deny I have a problem. My biggest problem is it shows. I gain weight. I have a bad complexion. I'm sluggish in everything. It shows so I can't get away with it. I wish I could.

Food has always been a problem for me. Mother stopped depriving me of food by the time I reached puberty. Whether it's because I was now as big as her or she just gave up trying, I may never know. All I know is she went from obsessing over my weight to total apathy. Either she doesn't remember or simply won't admit to it.

Food is a problem for my mother as well. During my teen years, she'd get extremely obese. Then I, too, would gain weight. I didn't gain as much as she did, still, there was no excuse for gaining so much. No longer deprived or reprimanded for overeating, I ate freely. It developed into a disorder that became a constant battle. Eight weeks of Overeaters Anonymous did absolutely nothing for me.

My Codependency therapist wants me to keep a food journal. I have to record what I eat, how I'm feeling at the time, and pertinent events to help me analyze my food issues.

The following entries record a few particularly stressful periods.

Jan 19: On the way home from group I stopped and bought three candy bars and ate them. Then bought three more to reward myself for going to group when I really wanted to stay in bed to escape depression. Plus I've been craving something sweet all day.

Jan 20 a.m.: One or more candy? Thought about stopping but feeling anxious about our financial situation. Worried about paying bills and having to decide if Joshua should go to kindergarten or stay in preschool, etc.

– 11:20 a.m.: Hungry–ate a banana. Not a lot of anxiety. Had quiet time.

– p.m.: Went to a banquet with Steve at church. Only had one plate. Chose coleslaw instead of potato salad. On the way home, we stopped at Eckerd's to pick up a birthday present and I bought a candy bar for each of us. Feeling sad that some friends had accepted a position in another church and would be leaving us. Feeling pressure to put on a jolly face for all the church people.

Jan 21 a.m.: Went to Codependency group. Had a very intense session. Stopped at a store and bought three candy bars. Ate them in my bedroom where Steve couldn't see. I deserved a reward for working so hard in group.

Feb 14 Valentine's Day: Ate a sugar-free candy bar and fruit for breakfast. Chose not to eat sugar. Got a lot of feelings about money. Prayed about my compulsive feelings toward my parents. Wrote a letter to my folks about Daddy's upcoming anniversary services.

Feb 15 a.m.: Ate breakfast. Took Joshua to school and returned home. Ate a small box of M&Ms from Josh's Valentine candy and two other pieces of candy. Feeling anxious about the letter I wrote to my parents. I'm afraid to send it.

– 10 a.m.: Made pudding with Nutrasweet. Ate some. Stopped and bought a hamburger and fries and a Diet Pepsi on the way to pick up sheet music from layaway at Stadium Bookstore. Got one candy bar when buying gas. Felt better after a snack.

– Picked Joshua up early from school to not be lonely on the way to the PMS doctor for a med refill. We sang songs and ate suckers. Stopped at a drugstore. Josh touched too many things. I wished I hadn't brought him. Bought SweeTARTS.

– Stopped to get gas. Bought Cheetos and honey-roasted nuts. Ate on the way home.

– Fixed dinner. Secretly ate pudding while cooking dinner. Ate dinner and felt stuffed. Feeling tense while eating.

Feb 16: Went to the drugstore late at night to buy a bar of soap. Thought it was a perfect time for candy but decided No! Enough is enough. Feeling lonely. Worried about losing the house. Preoccupied with parent issues.

Feb 17 a.m.: Breakfast: egg, toast and water. Did aerobics from a video. Felt good after exercising. Felt a little guilty about Tuesday but decided I could goof up once in a while. Today is a new day. Drank water. Had salad, green beans, and grilled chicken for lunch.

– p.m.: Hungry. Drank water. Thought about making salt-free popcorn. Feeling time pressure to get groceries, pick up Josh and supper, then group. Didn't eat.

– Went to visit a friend in the hospital, then to group. On the way home, bought hamburgers for supper. Came home and had a special time with Steve.

Notes From Codependency Group

I have a compulsion to numb my feelings. I overeat to rid myself of compulsions. Once the compulsion is satisfied, I feel I've accomplished my objective based on my false beliefs.

My False Beliefs

–Fat people get attention, both good and bad. Fat people are jolly.

–I never trusted a beautiful person. I thought they were ugly inside. That's an excuse I told myself to hide the fact that, in actuality, I'm jealous of thin people. I desire to be like them, but can't.

–I can't be sensual in any way because that equals sin. If I'm thin, I'll feel comfortable wearing pants which is immoral.

–Obesity is how I carry out my parents' moral convictions. Pastors' kids have to be different from everyone else. They have to set an example for the whole world. Good people are fat people. Thinness is associated with immorality and immodesty.

–I'm overweight like all the women in my family. Can't break traditional values or morals. Fat people are ostracized in our society. If I'm accepted by the world, I'm sinning because I'm associating myself with the world instead of Christ.

–Fat provides insulation I can hide behind. People repelled by fat people aren't going to try to get close to me. The risk of getting hurt by someone I have no relationship with is minimal.

Another Assignment

Reasons Why I WANT to Grow Up

- To carry out God's plan for my life
- To be emotionally mature for my age (Might as well. Right?)
- To complete my recovery
- To be an adequate mother
- To minister to others who are suffering
- To learn to cope with the reality of life
- To be at peace with myself and God

- To develop positive behavior changes
- To restore my sanity
- To reap the rewards of being mature

Reasons I DON'T Want to Grow Up

- Accepting responsibility
- Financial problems
- Too much pain and no fun
- Admitting defeats and failures
- Reality will replace the romance of living
- Having to face whoever I am (That's pretty scary.)
- Age equates to declining health
- No more daydreaming and living in a fantasy world (I'm not really sure I want to give this up.)
- Having more problems than I can face
- Having to deal with sorrow and grief

Inner Child

Little Girl

"I'm going to leave you," Mother screams.
No time for children, or so it seems.
"Daddy doesn't have time now," echoes in her mind.
She wishes she could find a way
to make the clock rewind
So they can sit and read together
or maybe they can play.
"I don't know when that will be, dear.
Perhaps some other day."
Run away, Daddy, run away from home.
By the time you return, Little Girl will be grown.

Run Little Girl, outrun the pain.
Reality's no good and there's nothing here to gain.
Hide behind the singer. Hide behind the mask.
Have a cookie. Dull the pain.
Though comfort never lasts.

Run, Little Girl, hide inside your head.
Nothing to fear and nothing left to dread.
Bury the pain away deep inside your heart.
Where no one can touch you or tear you apart.

I recall when we became friends, Little Girl,
The day I entered your sad little world.
"You work too hard. I need to play,"
you said with a frown.
I didn't listen, but you were right
and now we're spiraling down.
Perhaps I'll learn to listen
more closely to your heart.
Maybe then the two of us
will no longer fall apart.

> He will swallow up death for all time,
> And the LORD God will wipe tears
> away from all faces,
> And He will remove the disgrace
> of His people from all the earth;
> For the LORD has spoken.
>
> Isaiah 25:8 (NASB)

1992

Journal Entry

So very dry...why do I become spiritually dry when things are going well and I cling to the spiritual when I don't know what to do next? Why can't I be constant in whatever I'm doing, whether it's my relationship with my Creator, my neighbor, or my co-worker? I'm so off kilter...bumpy...inconsistent.

I feel pretty good now. Life is weird. Maybe I just think I'm dry when I'm actually okay. Maybe I expect to be on an emotional roller coaster all the time so when things are good it's unfamiliar and I think I'm not okay.

1993

Journal Entry

Played piano in the church choir room for about an hour and a half today. Cried and got out a lot of anger toward God and my parents. Forgave God for creating my dad and mom–for creating me.

Cried and cried as I poured out my soul through the music. I wish I could remember each note, each thought. But it was all in communication with God and then it was forgotten.

I began to forgive, and seek His comfort and strength. Began to play more prayerfully and had much more peace than in the beginning. Praised and worshiped Him. I felt one with Him. Prayers to find time alone with Him had been answered.

1994

Journal Entry

Sunday morning looms ahead like a dark ugly menace. To escape its clutches, I could stay beneath the quilt of deceit. But I must not. Integrity dictates I perform my duty regardless of circumstances. Oh, to be rid of this burdensome anchor chaining me to the approval of others. I promise myself it won't be for long.

It's been six years since I confronted my parents at Rapha. They refused to accept my boundaries then and when I wrote to them to establish boundaries during a visit, so I stopped trying to contact them. Although I miss them, I'm happy my family and I are free to live by our convictions.

Some time ago Mother called to inform us Daddy was in the hospital and we were obligated to visit so Junior and I went together. I didn't mind visiting so much, but didn't want to be alone with Daddy.

The visit could have provided an opportunity for finally making amends. Sadly, he played the victim role, expecting me to apologize for maintaining healthy boundaries. That didn't happen.

That was years ago and I haven't seen or heard from them since. Now Daddy is passing through on his way home from some ministry-related event. He wants to drop by for a visit. Mother isn't with him. I'm apprehensive about what to expect.

Journal Entry

Well, it's over! Daddy has come and gone. I wanted to cry tears of relief, but couldn't. Now they come, hesitantly, unsure what I'm feeling. Relief, joy, sorrow, anger, frustration, or a little of each? If tears came in colors–a color for each tear-producing emotion, mine would either form rainbow ribbons or become murky brown. Like when all the colors mix in the rinse water.

The house is quiet now. Peaceful, with regular night sounds. The radio is playing, the heater fan is blowing. Normal silence of home.

He looked good. I'm surprised how glad I was to see him. He's regained some weight after being ill and looks more like Daddy. His bones are no longer showing, his cheeks are no longer gaunt. Was he always so tall? How can I feel so much love for him and so much anger at the same time? I'm so confused.

He hugged me for a long time. He never hugged me much before. He was kind, but then, he only stayed for four hours. That didn't leave much time for conflict.

He looked at me for the first time and told me he saw a sparkle in my eyes and a glow on my face. I told him the Lord has been healing me. Tearfully, he said surgery had brought him closer to God than he had ever been. I sure hope that's true.

Oh, but Daddy, don't you want to hear about how I met Jesus? About the miracles He's given me? About my new relationship with Him? Why must everything be about you? Don't you see I, too, have a lot to offer? I have things to share. Am I a person to you? What do you see when you look at me? Do you see me at all or do you only see you?

Oh, Daddy, it's not good for me to be around you. You're intoxicating to me. I'm tempted to jump into the flytrap when you're so loving and kind. Why don't I trust you? I feel guilty because I'm so angry with you. My reality is shaken right now.

Who is this man? His dangerous tentacles of magnetism reach out to choke me back into codependency. Like that's gonna happen! I'm free. I passed the test this time! He's gone now!

Let me arise from the grave of entwinement with his identity.
I can't breathe if I remain closed up in that tomb.
Let me be free to breathe, to fill my lungs with the air of independence.

Free to soar-to try my wings on the winds of God's love.
Free to dream of wondrous things God wants for me.
Free to struggle and work through the nitty-gritty of everyday life to reach dreams.
Free to be me, an awesome spirit being very dear to the heart of God.
Free to hope God will one day complete the changes He wants in you, Dad.
I sincerely want Him to change me.

Journal Entry

My knee hurts. It's swollen like a grapefruit and looks puffy. I hate pain-physical or emotional. Did I do this to myself? Did I allow my emotional state to deteriorate to the point where my body is suffering the aftermath? I wish it was as easy as "thinking" myself well.

I have no control over this knee-yet I feel somehow responsible. I have no control over my parents' acceptance of me either. It's painful. They're in pain because they can't control me. I'm in pain because I can't control them. It's a vicious cycle. Control issues. I hate being out of control. It's such a helpless feeling. I don't like feeling helpless. There's nothing to cling to.

My father is a sick helpless old man, but the little girl inside of me sees him right up there with God. It hurts her to hear he could be wrong or fallible in any way. She longs for his smile and hugs. She wants to sit on his lap and have him sing and trot her on his knee. She wants him to accept her. But he won't. He has pounded his fist on the table, picked up his Bible, and turned away. She can't see his face. Are there tears-or just anger? Maybe there's both.

He left her again–just like he did so long ago when the house was dark. It was oh, so cold. She loved him fiercely, stubbornly. She clung to him, but he left her. Over and over again, he left her in the dark.

He left her with that woman. She was there, sitting in the dark in her rocking chair. The one whose eyes saw nothing. Felt nothing. Said nothing. Abandoned. Oh so long ago. And just yesterday.

I'm two and a half years old. My knees are growing inward. They put braces on me. I don't understand what these ugly metal things are. These shoes are ugly, too.

"Oh look, the corrective shoes look just like cowboy boots!" Mother encourages.

OOOooo cowboy boots! Yeah!

After an eternity, I am reprieved from daytime braces. I wear them only at night and I need to go to the bathroom.

"Mother, come help me!"

"Go back to your room, Faith!"

Why won't she come help me? It's dark. Braces won't let my knees bend and Mother won't help. She never wants to help me.

I need you, Mother! Please love me, Mother. I hope someday you have to wear braces just like mine!

Mother thinks I'm asleep as I carefully creep to the front porch and peek at her. She's sitting in a rocker–silently rocking back and forth. Creak-creak-creak. Back and forth–back and forth. It's too spooky–her rocking in the dark! I hightail it as quietly as possible back to the safety of my room and the comfort of my bed.

I am five years old.

"Mother, will you make some clothes for my dolly? She's all naked and feels cold." No new clothes for dolly.

"Why are you wearing that dress again? It has a hole in it. Can't you see it's all worn out?" Mother pokes her finger into the hole. It's my favorite dress. It has a bow to tie in the back and a gathered waist. It billows when I swirl!

"Mother, can you fix it?"

RRRRRIP! The hole is getting bigger and bigger! My heart races, I feel like she's tearing me in half.

"Mother, STOP!" RRRRRIP! It is torn completely off my body!

"Now get out of here and get some clothes on!"

I run out of the room bawling. Why did she do that? She could have patched it! She sews so many pretty things on the sewing machine! I know she could have patched it if she wanted to!

My favorite dress is gone. I hate her. I want my daddy home to protect me from Mother. Kind words are for outsiders, but her children get screamed at. Oh, Mother, how I wish you would speak kindly to me! Oh, Mother please be sweet!

Journal Entry

As part of therapy, I'm asked to read an article titled "Dear Little Girl." There are several phrases I identify with.

"...she cries out to be loved, and yet afraid..."

I'm afraid of abandonment, rejection, hate, and humiliation. I picture my mother's face with a look of disgust and anger toward me.

"...dreams of Easter bunnies and Prince Charming."

Let me become Alice from *Alice in Wonderland* or Beauty in *Beauty and the Beast*. Give me a fairy tale to live in because in them beasts are well defined and the story turns out well in the end.

"I need to love her...she is so overcome with sadness and deep hurt that even I can't reach her. Dear Little Girl who stands alone."

My little girl crouches all alone. She desperately needs someone to love her, cherish her, and acknowledge that she is there. To allow her to feel her feelings and validate her existence and the pain she feels. I don't know how to love her. I've been shoving her down inside, keeping her from being seen. Eating to feed her cry for nurturing. Trying to fill the emptiness of an abandoned soul.

"Sometimes it's so hard to let you feel this pain. I'd rather you be forever happy."

I tend to drift off into La-la land where the world is full of sunshine and all is happy and warm. To a place for thinking only happy, carefree thoughts. Looking through rose-colored glasses. And never looking down to see the defecation she's wading in.

"Little Girl, you ask me why?"

Over and over she asks why. To understand the reasons behind the pain. The reasons for the burning tears could be the key to my healing. Is there an unknown secret lurking in the corridors of my mind? What awful secret does she know that I'm afraid for her to share? Does some form of abuse she received have her wrapped in grave clothes? Are they binding her to the stench of wounds that will not heal? Creating a fragile child too immersed in pain to allow her to experience reality?

My Jesus, what is the answer?

Well, Little Girl, I don't know if I talked to you or nurtured you enough today or not. Sorry if I haven't. I feel completely drained.

Yep!

Guests are coming tomorrow.

Yippee!

I don't want them to come.

Why?

They'll know how we live, the filth we live in every day.

I don't care what they think.

Yeah, 'cause you're a little girl. You're not supposed to care. I'm a grownup and I should do better.

Let's play.

What? It's twelve-twenty-five a.m.!

Yes. I want to play, play, play. Let's play the piano.

Josh is asleep in the den. It'll wake him.

Oh pleeease?

Let's clean up the living room and dining table.

NO!

I have to. They're coming in the morning!

No-no-no-no! Un-uh! La-la-la-la–fingers in ears.

You're ignoring me!

Ha! You've been ignoring me all my life!

Ouch!

Let's play Barbies.

I don't want to play Barbies. I'll have to get up and go get her.

You don't care about me! Let's play the piano.

No! I'll think I have to sort all the music and dust it off. I can't play a dirty piano.

Dirt, dirt, dirt--too bad you can't see my face.

Oh!

And my hair.

Oooh!

And my fingernails. Laughs.

Worse than Josh's?

Much worse.

Dirty underwear?

Same ones for three days. Hee-hee.

AAAAH! Don't do this to me! You're trying to make me mad.

Hmm. What are we going to play? Hmm?

You know we can't play with Josh asleep right there on the floor.

You care more about Josh than you do me! Bleh! Sticking her tongue out.

I want to play too, but I'm concerned about waking Josh up. I'm his mommy and I have to take care of him.

You're my mommy, too, aren't you?

How about Barbie? Will you settle for one Barbie?

OKAY!

For some reason interacting with my inner child as though she's a separate individual comes naturally. I know of no other way to nurture her.

I haven't been faithful in keeping up with my journal. Group therapy and individual sessions with Dr. Kathy continue weekly as I process past and present issues, analyze disturbing dreams, nurture my inner child, and deal with personal and family problems.

I started having serious physical health issues this year, which has me going through all kinds of tests and exams to try to diagnose the symptoms. In the meantime, my doctor has treated me with steroids and various medications.

Needless to say, it's been a rough year.

Chronic Disease

Blissful Solitude

Gone.
They've gone and given me the gift of the day
to do as I please.
My favorite time.

Happy?
Are they content to go off without me?
I hope so.
I'm not their sole purpose for living–
responsible for their happiness.
They need to learn to have a life together–
father and son.
Both together and alone–
without my energy feeding them
each and every morsel like baby birds.

Angry?
Yes, I'm angry with them for being so needy.
I'm angry for all the energy they suck out of me.
They need a lot of help.
I used to do it all, but not now.
I'm tired. I refuse to be everything to them.
"Let me alone," I say. "Y'all go and play."
And I am content.

Lonely?
Naw. The radio keeps me company.
If I need a friend, all I have to do
is pick up the phone.
Please, God, let them stay gone forever.
At least until supper time.

Therefore, strengthen your feeble arms
and weak knees.
"Make level paths for your feet;"
so that the lame may not be disabled,
but rather healed.

Hebrews 12:12 (NIV)

1995

Last summer I was gardening in the backyard with Steve and my legs froze up. They began to shake as though I was having a seizure. My health continued to decline from there. Several months of medical testing finally produced a prognosis. The good news is I don't have a brain tumor. The bad news is I have a painful degenerative chronic disease that affects cognitive function and the nervous system. So much for deciding not to have more children to minimize the risk of getting sick.

Journal Entry

This is my first time entering data into the computer a friend gave me. It has finally come to pass...I have a computer in my house. Yes! Thank You, Lord, for providing the desires of my heart. I will attempt to do the article writing I've always dreamed of...maybe even write a book. Who knows?

It's hard to remember to write the new year in. I can't believe Christmas has come and gone. My tree is still standing in the den...gotta put it up.

I'm finally pretty much at peace with the chronic disease. However, it's a little maddening to feel great for a few days and start thinking perhaps the disease was never really there–then boom! I get a reminder. My face begins to tingle and twitch or my cognitive skills slow down and I can't think as fast as usual.

I've had a pretty good year so far. It's been almost two months since I've had a relapse. Trying new medical therapy seems to help. I have to remember to pace myself. To apply my newly developed skills to live with this disease until Jesus chooses to heal me.

God is the strength of my life. I thank Him for each day I feel well. May I remember He is my strength on days when I feel poorly.

The past few days have been pure agony. Chronic disease is like a giant magnet sucking all the energy from my body. Detoxing from three weeks of steroids has my mind completely deranged. I can't think coherently. My mind and emotions are pinging all over the place.

My eating consumption has launched to the moon. I'm as jittery as a cat walking on sticky paper and I'm extremely tense. I almost feel like I could throttle anyone who crosses my path–just because–and then weep over their demise. And my part in it. And then do it all over again.

Totally manic, I've tried calling just about everyone I can think of. Vivien was available every day for a while, but I think she was getting overwhelmed when she stopped taking and returning my calls. I finally got through to her and explained my situation. She arrived moments ago and is now sitting on my bed.

Steve called our music minister, Dan, and told him he needed help with me. He called Dan because being a Children's Choir director makes Dan the pastor over me. He showed up shortly after Vivien. He's here to support Steve.

"It's nice of you to come over, Dan," I say. "My pain level has been unbearable. I've called people to help me pray in the Spirit while waiting for a doctor to return my call, but I couldn't reach anyone. Even after leaving messages no one returned my call."

"That's because I asked people to make themselves less available to you," Dan calmly replies.

"YOU DID WHAT? WHY WOULD YOU DO THAT?" My temples throb as my blood pressure soars.

"It's for your own good and the good of your friends. You're on the phone too much."

"Well, it just so happens I talked to Ann from Dr. Kathy's office before you arrived. She commended me for reaching out and using the telephone when I was in so much pain! I need serious prayer cover! Isn't that what the church is for? Isn't that how we bear one another's burdens?"

"It wasn't my decision. It came from a higher authority."

"Pastor Des?" I'm shocked.

"No. Dr. Kathy. She said you were spending too much time on the phone."

"HOW DARE SHE! She cut me off and left town so I can't even reach her! That's just great!" Dan shrugs. I throw my hands in the air and stomp to my bedroom. Right when I need people most! I need God with skin on and everyone was told to back off? How could Kathy do that to me? I'm livid and I don't care who hears me rant about it.

It's called 'roid rage. It's not uncommon with the average one-week dose of steroids. The three full weeks my doctor prescribed for me is insane. I'm having terrible withdrawals as I detoxify. To add insult to injury, I also have incontinence.

"Look, Vivien!" I grab an adult disposable diaper and shake it at her. "Diapers! *Diapers*! I'm not a baby and I WON'T WEAR DIAPERS!" I hurl it across the room with all the force I can muster. I want to throw dishes. I want to smash things. Diapers are safe projectiles.

I snatch a pair of panties from a dresser drawer. "If I have to wear diapers I might as well put these to good use." I shove them on my head.

Josh is standing in his bedroom doorway across the hall from mine. I pass him as I stamp from my room boldly sporting lingerie headwear. He whispers loudly, "Vivien, what's the matter with my mom?"

"She's having a bad reaction to meds. She'll be okay once it gets through her system."

I ignore Dan loitering in our tiny living room as I stomp around the house raging. Steve follows like a cowering puppy. His feeble attempts to calm me are futile.

Eventually, all energy is swiftly sucked out of me. Fatigue hits as fast and furious as my previous temper tantrum. I'm finally calm. I remove my headwear and submit to prayer before everyone leaves. Exhausted, I collapse on my bed longing for a restful night's sleep. Wearing a wretched diaper.

Journal Entry

The past two or three days have been a living hell. Living with the pain of prednisone detoxification has my mind completely messed up. How long will this take? That is the question.

I desperately wanted my mother to come to help and support me during my relapse. She said she'll only come when I'm in bed and can't get up. Wow, Mom. Thanks a lot! My issues of abandonment and rejection rose up when I heard that. You know, I kind of want my mama
to take care of me when I'm sick.

God is good. He's given me a large church family to support me and care for me when I'm ill. He's my only source of hope when I'm so needy. It's a daily struggle to keep my emotions and attitude positive. I'm trusting Him to help me not cycle down to depression about my physical limitations.

Sometimes it just stinks! I want to scream and kick at the disease, but it's not a physical being I can defy with dignity and grace. Only God can make it happen. I really am a big baby about a lot of things and tend to whine through life.

Steve is so good to me and helps me as much as he knows how. My patience is not enough with him and Josh doing their part in housework. The house is very dirty and it really bothered me yesterday, but I knew I couldn't do it all. I almost have the bedroom organized. I'm finding the more organized I become, the less stressful my life is.

I think Dan is burned out taking care of me. He asked why I needed him to know and understand all the details of my disheveled life. The only thing I can figure out is I have somehow transferred my desire to win my dad's respect and acceptance to Dan.

Dan is out of his comfort zone big time. He's been stretched far beyond what he's used to as a music minister. God has to be the one to take care of him. I can't allow myself the luxury of worrying about him.

I'm hurt that he can't meet my unmet needs, but I realize no one human person can do that. Not Steve, not Dan, not anybody. Only God can meet those needs in me. That never-ending thirst for approval from my father. The quest hasn't ended. It goes on. We must find a way to stop it. It's insane. Only God knows how deep the threads run in my psyche. Only He can answer.

I've prayed for Dan more than once today. I feel somehow responsible for his present state of exhaustion. He also has another choir member who is suicidal. God, please let him allow professionals to help her. He lacks the training.

I've never felt lonelier in my entire life. I want someone to silently hold me. I don't want to have to talk. I want people. Yet, I only want quiet people who won't ask incessant questions and stare at me.

Journal Entry

Insidious, this disease.
Robbing me of confidence in almost everything.
Raping joy.
Confining me to limitations I despise.
Run. Run away from it.
You feel good today. Pretend it isn't there.
Slap! A wet mop of reality hits me in the face when I least expect it.
Like Mother's anger or Daddy's praise.
It doesn't think or reason, yet it has a mind all its own.
Own it or not, I struggle to deny that anything's wrong.

My body cheers for the other side.
"Traitor!" I scream, "You're supposed to be on my side!"
"I always cheer for the winning team," it says with a shrug.
I grit my teeth. The scream wanting to escape becomes a growl.
No sense in kicking anything. No energy to waste.
Just let it ride. Ride where you hide.
It doesn't particularly matter anymore.
You've become a whining witch.

Whatever happened to the fight to not give in?
Why have you given up?
Don't you know the good man never gives in?
Never compromises?
Always stays on top of it, no matter what it takes.
You are a weakling. Ha. I've got you now.
You'll never amount to anything, never succeed at anything.
Be positive. Go on trying. Fighting is in vain.
You know it. Just admit it.

Run away.
Hide–but it's still with you, cursing the person you used to be.
Slowly creeping to control more and more of your life every minute.

Oh, keep reading books on various and often conflicting remedies.
Keep on thinking you'll exercise tomorrow.
Just try to stay on that diet.
You know it's impossible, but it'll give you something to do.
It's really no use.

What kind of contribution can you make now?
What damage has been done to your mind that you're unaware of?
How can you trust your rationale ever again?
No, you are not mad, but you may as well be. You'd be better off.
In the madness, you won't have to deal with it.
That's it! Run and hide in the corners of your mind. Away from everybody.
Not good enough? Colorado won't do it, nor Hawaii.
It's with you wherever you go, even in the backyard.

Journal Entry

"Is not this the kind of fasting I have chosen, to loose the chains of injustice and untie the cords of the yoke, to set the oppressed free and break every yoke? Is it not to share your food with the hungry and to shelter the poor wanderer–when you see the naked, to clothe them, and not turn away from your flesh and blood? Then your light will break forth like the dawn, and your healing will quickly appear; then your righteousness will go before you, and the glory of the Lord will be your rear guard."
– Isaiah 58:6,7 (NIV)

I haven't studied this passage as a Bible scholar would. All I know is what it means to me. GOD IS GOING TO HEAL ME!!! I have obeyed His voice and He loves me and He is going to heal me–SPEEDILY! By His Word, I am healed in the name of Jesus! Praise His name.

There's gonna be some shouting HALLELUJAH! And all the little children will grow up to tell their children and grandchildren what they witnessed to the glory of God the Father. IN THE NAME OF JESUS I AM HEALED. Now we wait for the body to line up with the word of the Lord. Amen.

Journal Entry

God says to bring the hungry and forsaken into our home and to feed and clothe them. He sent us just such a person only a few weeks ago. Isn't God good?

I met Tim at the bus stop one day, invited him to church, and shared a tract with him. We visited with each other on the bus and I advised him on how to deal with the community hospital where he was headed. Now he is almost like a member of the family. We all love him and feel blessed that he is a friend.

Journal Entry

I feel better, but so what? That doesn't change the facts about a lot of things. Like Children's Choir for instance. Am I going to start back soon, or am I going to start back at all? And what about church? Am I going to want to go back?

This morning I read the last couple of verses in Isaiah 58. It said to honor the Sabbath and not to do what I want to do, but to do what God wants me to. But I can't hear His voice like I did when I was psychotic. I desperately want to hear it as I did then. He was so close, so real. There was never any doubt in my mind about Him or what He was saying to me.

He told me He was going to heal me. There were conditions, but I believed He would do it. So is He? And why hasn't it happened yet? Is it up to me? Or is it up to Him? Or is it a combination of the two? I know I can't do any of this without His grace and power. Does everyone experience this? Or is it just me?

On the flip side, frustrating as cognitive challenges are, I can't help but laugh at some of the crazy stuff that comes out of my mouth. Like the time I told Josh to put his laundry in the freezer or told him to get his feet on instead of his shoes.

Sometimes I have difficulty thinking of the right word for simple everyday items. I have to come up with alternatives like the dog being a "bark maker" or a broom a "sweepy thingy." It frustrated me to no end at first, but now I laugh with everyone else.

Not so funny is not being able to recognize or recall the names of people I've known for years and see often. I'm not the only one with this problem. Others in my chronic disease group and I have deemed anyone we can't place at the moment as Barbara or Bob.

Journal Entry – 4 a.m

Can't sleep. Woke up. Dozing brain.
Problem solving, running fast.
I don't feel like writing but need to anyway.

Meryn from choir came and washed dishes yesterday while I slept. She was such a breath of fresh air! She didn't get my iron skillets very clean, but still, I'm grateful for the help. I wonder what she thought about us doing dishes by hand. Or seeing all the filth. Or seeing for the first time what we do and don't have. Now what does she think of me? Still, the church family is very supportive. I'm so glad I reached out to ask for help.

I want to be gracious and humble when people come to help. Humility is something I evidently need to experience and acquire. There's such a fine line! Hard to distinguish between shame and humility. I'm so afraid of taking advantage of people kind enough to help.

Jesus is working with me to face fears, selfishness, and shame. To be more transparent so He can be seen more clearly through me. Gosh, I need wisdom!

I expect too much from Steve. He's so good to me. Thank you, God, for Steve. He's the best human thing that ever happened to me.

Josh is worried about me. God, I love this kid. I suspect he may be jealous of the new baby–a puppy. What to do? He's so sensitive–like his mommy. He's brilliant, too. Also, like his mommy. Gosh, such a challenge. Like this life.

Different Voices

♪ Does Anybody See? ♪

Huddled in the corner,
her knees drawn to her chest,
A little girl sits cowering away from all her fears.
Life goes on around her. Life she doesn't see.
Reality consumes years of questions
Asked only through her tears.

Does anybody see? Does anybody care?
I'm afraid to let you see the pain I feel inside.
Please won't you see? Won't somebody care?
Won't you see the teardrops shining in my eyes?

Standing in the courtyard, His eyes turned to see
The crowd as they wished upon Him death.
Through all their ugliness only He could see
The anguish they felt within their souls.
And with love, He laid His body down to die.

"Please won't you see who I am?
I am Jesus who for you was crucified."
Kneeling in His presence, she clings to the throne,
He gazes down with loving eyes.
"I've carried you through your suffering.
See, I'm holding on to your hand.
I want you to see through your fears
and to understand
Yes, I see you. Yes, I care!

"I see your pain and the fear you have inside,
Please won't you see who I am?
I am Jesus who for you was crucified.
And I see the teardrops shining in your eyes."

> But you are a chosen generation,
> a royal priesthood, a holy nation,
> His own special people,
> that you may proclaim the praises of Him
> who called you out of darkness
> into His marvelous light;
> who once were not a people
> but are now the people of God,
> who had not obtained mercy
> but now have obtained mercy.
>
> 1 Peter 2:9-10 (NKJV)

1995

Journal Entry

Daddy passed away. Leukemia or some sort of blood disease. It's been hard realizing that he is gone. I often dream that he's not really dead. One dream was about him staging his death so he could become a superhero to save the world. It was ridiculous, but showed how angry I was at him for dying. Another dream was similar. I can't remember details at the moment, but again, he wasn't dead. Guess I'm still in denial. To what percentage, I'm not sure.

"Daddy died. They buried him far, far away in the snow.

"You're so stupid, you'll never amount to anything.

"If only you'd lose a little weight, I think you'd be quite attractive.

"Get your act together, others are watching.

"You screamed at Josh yesterday. Do you think the neighbors heard?

"Okay, Show Time! Put on that happy face. Time to go play the church organ.

"She doesn't like me. I could feel it in the vibes around us. What can I do?"

I stop speaking and look up at Dr. Kathy. "What's the matter, Doctor? You have that look on your face again."

"Am I hearing different voices?" Dr. Kathy asks.

"What are you talking about? No way! How could you even suggest such a thing? I'm just sharing my thoughts at the moment!"

"It's okay if you don't want to face it now. The mind has a way of revealing things when you're ready to face them. We can wait. The mind is so amazing. If we can't handle the emotional trauma of memories, it won't show up in our psyche until it is time to face it."

"Why is this pain so intense? Will it always be this way?"

"You can receive healing through God and therapy without the details of all the abuse."

"I beg your pardon?"

"Psychology tests indicate your maturity level seems to alter at different times."

"Huh?"

"You were a little child when you prayed a moment ago."

"I'm confused."

"I'd like to use guided imagery with you."

"I don't think so!" I shudder at what we might unearth.

"It's probably not at all what you're imagining. I want to help you relax, to go deep within yourself. You'll be aware and will remember everything. I can teach you how to achieve it on your own."

"Okay, if that's all it is!"

"I promise. Now I want you to relax. Imagine we're in a house, walking down a flight of stairs together. There is a door at the bottom of the stairs. I want you to open it. Tell me what you see."

"The stairway before us is long and dark. I can't see the bottom. The only light is from behind us. The house we're in is a huge monstrosity, like in horror movies.

"The door at the bottom of the stairs opens into a long hallway. Both walls are lined with many dimly lit gas sconces separated by closed doors. I try each door, but they're locked. We approach the last door at the end of the hall. I open it and peer inside. It's hard to see because heavy drapes are drawn."

Out of the corner of my eye, I notice movement. "What's that?" Looking closer, "I see a very frightened small child sitting on a dusty floor. Her clothes are soiled. Her hair is matted. She cowers with filthy arms wrapped around drawn legs."

"What is your name?" Dr. Kathy asks the child. The child is speechless.

"She appears to be afraid of someone."

"Can we light a candle for you?" No reply. Dr. Kathy lights a candle stuck in a brass holder. The child seems confused, but her eyes glow with curiosity and delight at the warm wick.

Satisfied with what she sees, Dr. Kathy says, "We need to go, but we'll be back. Don't look so sad, we'll be back, I promise." We pray for angels to surround the child's room and slowly climb the stairs.

"The little girl in the room is your inner child," Dr. Kathy explains. "Why do you suppose she may be in that room?"

"I'm not really sure."

"What do you feel when you're with her?"

"Great sadness. Abandonment."

"We will need to nurture her and check in on her upon occasion. Are you willing to do that?"

"Yes."

Returning to the room, we find the candle is still lit. Dr. Kathy addresses the child while I observe. "Look, We've brought you a new white dress. Let's get you cleaned up so you can wear it. I need to open the drapes so sunshine can come in." The little girl shields her eyes against the blinding light. "Look what else we brought you, a beautiful canopy bed!"

"Oooh!"

"Will you tell me your name?"

"It's Alisa. Will you play with me?"

"Sure. Would you like to go outside?"

She sadly hangs her head. "I'm not allowed."

"What are you afraid of?"

"The lady with the big shoes."

"It's okay. You'll be safe with us. We'll just go out for a short time and come right back. Okay?"

"Okay."

"Alisa, we have a surprise for you. We're going to take you to a carnival. You can have cotton candy, lollipops, and hot dogs! And there will be other children to play with, too."

"That sounds like lots of fun! Let's go."

"Wait!" I say. "Someone else is here. She's a young teenager."

"I wonder who this could be," Dr. Kathy asks.

"I'm Daphne.

"I'm Alisa. We're going to a carnival, wanna join us?

"Sure."

After a fun time together the carnival adventure ends. We lead Alisa and Daphne toward the big house.

"Let's make you a little house to play in," suggests Dr. Kathy.

I visit Alisa from time to time and notice she is blossoming and growing. Without telling Dr. Kathy, I decide it's time to blow up the big house and let Alisa live in the little one we created for her. Alisa is all for that idea. We blow up the spooky old house and dance and laugh until the smoke clears. Alisa enters her playhouse.

I climb up the hill toward my conscious mind. As I look back at the charred remains it seems as though I see several children peeking out from mounds of rubble. Are there more? Should I have kept the house? What have I done?

Images of those children haunt me. I've been trying to push them out of my mind. I blew up the house, so anything or anybody else was surely blown up as well. Right?

Continuing our work with Alisa over time, I realize she has become a young lady whose fears have gone. She no longer needs Dr. Kathy or me, so we leave her there in her little house. I haven't seen her since. This, I'm told, is called integration. When a personality is healed they integrate.

While Alisa has integrated, Daphne has become more prominent. She has serious performance issues that lead to depression stemming from my (our?) parents. I've begun to have vague and disturbing memories of being very young and getting molested by a man from church who was a friend of the family and by my grandfather. Apparently, these memories are coming from Daphne. I hate them. They weigh heavily on me, causing great distress and emotional turmoil.

Journal Entry

I wish Jesus would change His mind about me staying in life. He takes such good care of me here, how much more splendid it would be to live with Him forever.

I'm so tired.
Tired of the pain.
Tired of the constant turmoil.
Tired. Just tired.

Right now it feels as though it doesn't matter anymore. It would be better if I was with Jesus. He's the only One for me. He's the one way out of this madness. He's the only One who loves me where I am–in the madness, the tiredness, wherever I am, He's there. He's the only One who can rescue me from this insidious existence. His perspective is the only one that matters.

"Dr. Kathy speaking."

"Hello, Dr. Kathy. This is Daphne. I'm feeling really low." Tearfully, "I no longer want to live. I'm having suicidal thoughts."

"Where are you?"

"I'm at a pay phone downtown."

"Listen, I want you to drive to the hospital and check yourself in. Will you do that for me?"

"Yes."

"Good. I'll call Steve and have him take your toiletries and essentials to you."

I'm laying on a hard hospital bed trying to sleep. Every time I've attempted to leave my room for any reason I'm sent back to bed.

Patients here are unnerving. People shuffle the halls in a fog of despair. There's a woman who refuses to eat until her son arrives from another state. An old man roams the hallways playing with his genitals. Worst of all is the woman who had a leg amputated and screams day and night in Spanish.

Dr. Kathy told me Daphne is the one who is suicidal, but this hospital doesn't deal with DID issues. How can they help me deal with suicidal thoughts if they're not mine, but Daphne's?

I'm not sure how much better I am, but after two and a half weeks I'm released. I'm now able to resume therapy with Dr. Kathy.

"Will you talk to me, Daphne? Faith said it was alright with her. I know you're hurting and I'd really like to help you."

"Dr. Kathy, Daphne is really in a bad place right now. She can't talk to you. She is terrified that you'll tell the preacher you found her and that she'll be abused again."

"It's okay if you don't talk to me today, Daphne. We will never reveal your hiding place. Faith tells me that you need some rest, some alone time–where you do not have to perform.

"Faith, let's make Daphne a little cottage by the sea. We'll give her a piano if she wants to play it. She can take a vacation from anyone listening."

"Okay."

"Now, Daphne, there will be protection for you. Not bodyguards, but your cottage can only be reached by crossing over a small bridge. An angel at the gate won't allow anyone unauthorized to cross. Do you think you'd like that, Daphne?"

"I think she does. She's calmer now, sitting on the beach watching the sea."

"Is she still suicidal?"

Shrug. "She's not really communicating to me, but I would guess she feels a lot safer now. I don't know, though. Sometimes I get tired of fighting and think maybe she's right."

"She's right?"

"Yes, about us being better off dead."

"Do you believe that, Faith?"

"No..." I whine. "But I am getting tired here. She keeps telling me stuff I never knew happened to me–her–whatever!"

"Has Daphne revealed a memory to you?"

"Yes and no." I pause, wondering how to explain. "Well, it was kind of a flashback or a dream. Remember I told you my grandfather molested me on occasion? He did, but Daddy looks a lot like him." I start crying. "Daphne revealed that Daddy molested her from the time I was about five years old until she–you know–started the monthly thing. Not grandpa, *Daddy!*"

"Oh, I am so sorry, Faith and Daphne. This never should have happened to you. How awful."

I wring my hands. "Dr. Kathy, is any of this real? Are these really memories? It sounds like something made up. It's all so horrific and confusing."

"When you think of this memory, do you see it happening? Where are you when he's touching you?"

"I'm watching."

"Like you are above, looking down?"

"Yes, but also like it's happening to me, too. It's weird."

"It doesn't sound weird to me at all. Memories can be that way sometimes."

"But he *couldn't* have done it!"

"Perpetrators often have a good side and a very dark side. That's how they keep from getting caught most of the time. The children are frightened into silence and the abuser shows a good, holy, upstanding citizen side to the world."

"It's so hard to believe."

"Yes, it is. This may also explain why your alters waited for so long to emerge. It wasn't safe to do so when your father was alive."

"He would have denied it."

"I'm sure he would have. And who would people believe, you or him?"

"Him."

"Most likely."

"What if there's more?"

"What? More abuse?"

"More people."

"You mean more personalities?"

"Yes."

"Well, right now let's just work on Daphne, okay? If you have other people they won't reveal themselves until you're ready."

"Really?"

"Yes, that's just the way it happens. You've had Daphne all this time, ever since you were abused, but you didn't know or remember the abuse until your mind was ready to work on it."

"So I can't just make this stuff up, can I?"

"Why would you want to?"

"I see your point. Why have junk like this to deal with on top of everything else?" Sigh. "What if I don't want to work on it?"

"You could choose not to, but at some time or another, these issues will resurface again and then you'll have to deal with it. You may as well face it now. You have always worked hard in therapy. I believe you can do it. And I'll be right here to help you."

"I feel like a freak."

"Oh no, no. On the outside, no one notices anything different. That's the beauty of having different personalities. They all work at holding you together so you appear to be normal and carry on your daily business as usual.

"You know, Faith, it takes a highly creative person with above-average intelligence to develop this system. It's a way of coping. You split off when you couldn't deal with the horrendous abuse. A child can only deal with so much on a regular basis. That's when the mind and creativity help you split to dissociate from the abuse."

"So what do I do now?"

"Just let things slowly come to the surface. Journal any dreams you have and write, write, write. Write your feelings about all this. Perhaps Daphne will want to write, also. That would be great."

"Okay. Thank you, Dr. Kathy. See you next Tuesday."

Several alters have become known to me this year. Once I become aware of them, we begin to interact among ourselves. Dr. Kathy refers to this as my "system." For the most part, we all get along–almost like companions. However, a rebellious teenage boy alter named Joey tends to goof off too much and agitates an older male alter, Nathan, who'd like to deck him from time to time. And to be honest, I'm not particularly fond of Daphne. I'd just as soon she keep her morbid memories, depression, and teenage issues to herself.

Sometimes all of this freaks me out. It blows my mind to discover that not all of the conflicting voices constantly rambling in my head for as long as I can remember were my parents', but also alternate personalities. What's even more disturbing is that I accept it. At least most of the time.

Journal Entry

Denial, hello!

I've often felt like a chameleon, changing with the environment. It just occurred to me that Dissociative Identity Disorder (DID) is very similar to that. From the time I was young, I played as a child when with other children, but when with older people I'd act mature. Likewise, when with African Americans I talk and act like them. I'm essentially all things to all people.

So here's the question, do I actually have DID, or am I merely adapting to my surroundings as a chameleon? Do I have multiple personalities or am I using it as a distraction from my problems? Ever since I acknowledged having DID a whole bunch of alters have emerged, making them annoyingly visible to the world.

I want to deny they exist, but they're too real to me. Memories-their memories-ones I didn't recall before are too intense and much too painful for me to ignore or dismiss.

Memories of the past-are they real? I relive experiences once hidden through dreams as "body experiences." They're too great a confirmation. But why now? Why, after all these years are these memories all of the sudden attacking me? If these personalities have been with me all this time, why show up now? Just stay buried in my mind's graveyard so I can move on with my life. Deny their existence.

Work with Dr. Kathy continues to uncover more personalities. Each conceals their own ugly secret of trauma or abuse. I think I'm really cracked! I don't want to find more personalities! It scares me. Why do I have to face it, anyway?

Dr. Kathy tells me the only way to recovery is straight through the pain-to walk into the fire and face it. But what if none of this is true? What if it never happened? What if I'm making it all up? After all, I am creative. Maybe I'm fabricating all this to avoid facing daily life.

Dr. Kathy says if I can handle life without these things coming up-by all means-do it. God created the mind to address issues when I'm capable of doing so. So we work-inch by inch-millimeter by millimeter. I can't do this! Help!

God is here even though I am often unaware. He is here.

Journal Entry

> In the beginning, was the Word, and the Word was with God, and the Word was God. He was with God in the beginning. – John 1:1 (NIV)

Tonight at Bible study the Holy Spirit showed me an amazing fact in my recovery. Jesus was there in the beginning–whenever that was.

Daphne had recently remembered another horrible thing Daddy did to us when we were young. Jesus was there with me before the sexual abuse occurred and with Daphne and me while it was happening.

Tonight–in a few seconds, Jesus helped me see and understand that He was there. He was crying very sorrowfully over what was happening. He knew beforehand that it was going to happen so He gave me the ability to split at the time of the abuse!! Having multiple personalities is a gift instead of the insanity Satan would have me believe.

Thank You, Jesus, for revealing this to me. I know it's very important for me to grasp.

If You were there giving me the gift to split into different personalities, then You are here and will give me the gift of merging them back together!!! It all seems so elementary, but it's not during therapy–or when a new memory or personality is emerging!

Lord, it just plain hurts. But now I have a glimmer of hope. Praise Your name. Help me walk it out, Father. Please hold my hand, Jesus, like You did when I was manic. You were so real to me then. I could feel Your presence and knew Your voice even with all the other voices inside of me.

I'm not into Your Word and not walking with You like I was then. I desperately clung to You then because You were the only One who understood me. I'm obviously not trusting

You like I did during that difficult time. Oh, Jesus, forgive me for my sin! Help me walk with You each day.

I need You, Jesus. I need so much love right now. None of my friends or my family can ever give me enough hugs and kisses. Lord, I need You to hold me as You've done so many times before. I need hugs and kisses from You Jesus.

Each person inside me has their own set of sins and shortcomings. Please forgive us of our sins, of our selfishness and pride, of always wanting to do things our way.

Thank You for Dr. Kathy. Please give her extra insight. Guide her, Lord. You are the only One who can bring me wholeness.

Help me trust You, Lord. Amen.

My System of Alters

Smile Little Dolly

Smile, little dolly, and don't wrinkle your dress.
Sing a song. Give a speech. Be sure to impress.
Company is coming, put on your happy face.
Make them love you. Cause me no disgrace.

Smile, little dolly. You will never know
How much of me is entwined within your little soul.
Learn to make them laugh. Learn to please the lot.
You're my precious dolly. The only one I've got.

Where are you, little dolly? Why did you run so fast?
I could never understand why you were so depressed.
I wish I could fix you and see you do a dance.
But now I'm fairly certain
I'll never get the chance.

The LORD replies,
"I have seen violence done to the helpless,
and I have heard the groans of the poor.
Now I will rise up to rescue them,
as they have longed for me to do."

The LORD's promises are pure,
like silver refined in a furnace,
purified seven times over.

Therefore, LORD, we know
you will protect the oppressed,
preserving them forever
from this lying generation,
even though the wicked strut about,
and evil is praised throughout the land.

Psalm 12:5-8 (NLT)

1996

Journal Entry

Awake, awake, Zion, clothe yourself with strength! Put on your garments of splendor, Jerusalem, the holy city. The uncircumcised and defiled will not enter you again.
– Isaiah 52:1 (NIV)

It's Sunday morning and I'm planning on going to the House of God! What a fitting scripture, put on my strength (Jesus). Wake up and put on my strength (our Daily Bread), the Word of God! Then, after I've plugged my tea kettle into my Power Source (Jesus) put on my beautiful garments and get ready to go to the House of God!

Jesus tells me, *Put on something pretty just for Me. I enjoy lovely fabrics. Get all dressed up just for Me and let's go together to My House! Yes, come over to My House. There's going to be a party in My honor and I just can't wait to bless you over at My House. I have prepared a feast just for you. You will be pleased! For the feast I have prepared will awaken your taste buds, tease your palette, and leave you craving more!*

Wow! And what a wonderful feast it was! Went down to be prayed for. Figured if the Lord had told me He was going to heal me that it might as well be this Sunday. Or any time, really. I'm ready!

The Holy Spirit showed up and I don't remember much except that I was being loved on by the Lord and I was loving Him back.

But now I feel so frustrated.

Steve was really grouchy this morning helping me get ready for church. He snapped at me several times and questioned everything I wanted to take with me. I had given it all a lot of thought beforehand, but I hadn't bothered to let him in on the details, so he freaked out on me. As it is, I forgot to grab a handkerchief.

I was feeling stressed because he was upset and not having a good morning. His anxiety kind of made me want to hurry and get ready, which stressed me out. I just don't do "hurry" well at all. He knew when I got up at 3:30 this morning that the hypomania was kicking in.

I was excited about going to church. I wanted to be ready on time but was still running late so I applied makeup on the way. It turned out well because the lighting was excellent and I didn't feel rushed. I went in just before the last song and got to hear the choir sing "Oh How Sweet the Name." It was wonderful.

Steve was rather embarrassed because I was very loud in church. I went forward for anointing and he freaked out when I was shouting and screaming and loving Jesus in my spirit. He also thought I was too loud during the sermon and hallelujahed and amened way too much. Even though we've been in a charismatic church since leaving the Baptist church years ago, he still has issues accepting the Pentecostal Spirit-thing so I think he got confused as to who was making all that noise. I apologized to him and told him I'd tone it down. This will not discourage me from loving my Jesus in His house.

We had a fight about it after we got home. Since I had been so emotional and the steroids had me pinging off the walls he had a hard time believing the commotion was caused by the Holy Spirit and not me. I reminded him that in the flesh I don't like attention, and that this whole situation was rather attention-getting. But to be honest, I didn't really care because it was a rare and beautiful gift from the Holy Spirit.

I am sad, though, that I embarrassed the love of my life who has been so great to me. He truly has been a sweetheart through this past exacerbation. I told him he takes on my chronic disease too much. Maybe he needs a break from taking care of me. I think that would be nice.

Anyway, Devil, in the name of Jesus, get out of my house. You have no business here. Go! Get out from around my husband and son in Jesus' name! His blood covers us so stop saying things to Steve that are not true.

Father, please help Steve understand I need to do as much for myself as I can and that it takes away my dignity when he does everything for me. Please grant me understanding and compassion and Father, please help Steve have a new and truthful perception of things in his mind. Bless his heart. Lord, he really sees things very crooked sometimes.

I love You and I'm so glad You are on my team. Thank You in advance for working out this little bump in our journey together. Please give Steve peace and let his anxiety no longer exist. Please let me guard my tongue and my sound level. Let me enjoy You fully without ruining the service for Steve. Oh, Jesus, I just love You and know that I want to love You forever.

I'm Annie and I'm four years old.

The mother is really mean! She locks me up in a closet and won't let me eat because I'm fat and ugly. She doesn't want me to look pretty for Daddy.

She shut me up. In a box and even in a 'fridge-rater one time. I couldn't breathe. It was so scary that now whenever I get in closed-in places or if it's too hot in a room, I feel like I can't breathe. I don't like closed-in places. 'Specially if it's dark.

I'M HUNGRY, MAMA! I WANT HAMBURGERS AND MOUNTAIN DEW!

Like any other four-year-old, Annie needs guidance in developing healthy eating habits and using her indoor voice.

I'm feeling too disoriented to drive to group today. Will you please drive for me, Joey?

You bet! Thanks! Hey, how about a cigarette?

No.

Can I have a candy bar, Mama?

I'll consider it.

Journal Entry

Lots of things going on in what I've come to accept as my system of personalities. Dr. Kathy wants me to do the same in DID group as I do during our private therapy sessions.

Today in group, Maymee came out to talk and sing. On the way home I began to doubt this multiple thing again. Group therapy seems to be working–but I wish I hadn't let Maymee out–most embarrassing!

Group members were supportive, but I'm the only one of a group of people with DID who's had any alter come out to talk. Each of them refers to their people, but so far I haven't experienced any of them letting any of their people talk. Am I doing something wrong?

Letting Maymee talk shook the system up. Did I make her up? Does she really exist? Can she sing like I want to sing deep down? Was I just acting–playing a part?

The group wants to hear her sing next week. Of course, Maymee complied. It appears that I have a choice to make a big deal of this or just let it be. The thing about it is, her acceptance means a lot to me. I wish it didn't.

Journal Entry

Used to keep my diary on the computer until the computer crashed. Told my friend Vivien about having DID. At her recommendation, I've resumed keeping a journal. Thanks, Viv.

Yesterday Steve lost his job at the freezer warehouse.

Occasionally feeling the effects of the chronic disease I was diagnosed with last year. So far it's been manageable with medication. Dealing with emotional pain sure doesn't help matters!

Dr. Kathy told me it's uncommon for alters to interact with each other the way mine do. She encouraged me to draw a picture of the world inside my mind. It flows from me without having to think. The pencil moves and images emerge.

Two strange creature-looking things are imprisoned for my protection. I've surrounded the cell with angelic soldiers.

Below the cell is a group of round heads with shoulders. The larger image represents my mother leading her army. The likeness of Adolph Hitler in the box on the top right is also part of her army.

Four personalities are represented on this page. Directly below Hitler, Maymee is pictured with full lips, short wavy hair, and looped earrings. I wasn't aware of it at the time, but she's the one who embarrassed Steve during a church service when she emerged. I wasn't aware of it at the time, but she's the one who embarrassed Steve during a church service when she emerged. She nurtures and protects me like a loving mother.

Nathan is a carpenter. His blond hair is cut in a military butch. He's the system bodyguard and has big muscular arms which he shows off by wearing a tight tee shirt. He makes threats but everyone else keeps him in check. He provides the muscle to whatever the system wants most. If we need and want protection, he'll give it. If he needs to help save our lives, he'll do that. However, if there's a unanimous death wish, he'll also facilitate that.

Joey is a muscular teenager with dark hair who speaks with a hint of a Spanish accent. Straight shoulder length, it falls over one eye. He wears black leather, and occasionally, a black headband, boots, and gloves with partial finger coverings. He'd like to smoke and drink and maybe even take drugs if I let him. He likes to drive very fast. He also likes to kid around, which causes a lot of friction between him and Nathan.

Annie is a small girl with short, straight hair. She's drawn from head to toe, but her only features are her big round eyes and two dots on her chest. She has no clothes, hands, or feet. She likes to play tricks on Joey. I'm pretty sure she emerged during a meltdown while I was coming off of steroids.

My daddy has an army pictured in a second illustration. Both my parents' armies are forces designed to control me.

Iris is drawn as an outline of a short, curly-haired girl in a triangle dress with stick legs. She's the Gatekeeper who organizes the system, arranging who is out front and what alters are to be doing. She's young, but organized and occasionally bossy.

Daphne has a heart-shaped face, dark eyes, and very long curly hair. She's a performer and perfectionist. There are two Daphnes, a child, and a teenager. Young Daphne is not pictured.

Melissa also has long, very curly hair and a voluptuous figure. She's married to Steve. Melissa enjoys sex with Steve. She also likes computers.

There's an animal that looks like a dog, but it's actually a demon pig. He's bound at Dr. Kathy's suggestion so he can't do any harm. I've drawn a playground for the children to play in. I've surrounded them with angels to protect them so they won't be afraid.

Holding
7 cells
Dad's
army
IRIS
Daphne
Melisa
playground for
children

I've drawn a third illustration of the system. It includes images of Mother's and Daddy's armies and adds a playroom for children and Annie, who is now clothed. A safe-house cottage by the sea has been added for Daphne. Maymee is taking Daphne and Faith there in a boat for respite. This allows another alter to "come out front" and take control without conflicting issues. Maymee was out front at the time of this drawing.

Journal Entry

I have one ear to the TV while writing in my journal. The preacher reminds me of a couple of good qualities of my dad. He's probably about the same age Daddy was when he passed away last year.

This preacher has a little more polish and style than Dad. There are similarities in their gestures, wording, and delivery of a sermon. I find it too distracting. I better change the channel.

Poor tenor! His talent is the only thing that gives that duet any redeeming quality! The alto is singing flat, and obviously above her natural range. Tenor almost winces as she delivers a solo part.

You'd know, Daphne. You've performed enough to recognize perfection though you've never quite achieved it yourself.

Our church choir has performed this song. It is a demanding arrangement. This choir uses a soundtrack. It blares out the absence of a live orchestra. How spoiled we are at Bethesda.

Daddy would admonish them and put them on a guilt trip for taking things for granted.

I have an overwhelming desire to preach at them–to rant and rave–like Daddy did.

Either a new person is emerging or the core person is becoming stronger. Daphne would have us all merge into her–because she has all the best skills and intellect. Or so she thinks.

There's a haughty Daphne who is arrogant and a pain in the rear. There's a hurting Daphne who remembers sexual abuse and needs a lot of love. She's extremely dependent on our church music minister, Dan, for affirmation.

It's appalling to discover how demanding and impossible Daphne has been to people. I apologize to a couple of people over and over. They're gracious. But it hurts like hell.

The Holy Spirit has shown me I need to be a servant. He's convicted me of an underlying attitude towards a certain person at church. This has been ongoing for several months.

Please forgive me, Father. Please make me clean again, even though it is mostly Daphne who has this attitude and must repent. I must take responsibility because she is me and I am she. What a mess!

We should gain ground as Daphne matures and learns to obey the Master. She bears a lot of abuse from the daddy. She has several issues with him.

Realizing each person inside me has their own set of beliefs, sins, faults, and shortcomings is overwhelming. Each either doesn't know the Lord or they have their own personal walk with Him.

Please, Lord, forgive my complaining, but it all seems to slowly creep along. Except for that week that memories were coming way too fast. Whew! Only You know what's best. Please guide our therapy today. Please give Steve understanding.

Mental illness sucks. I'm reminded of my mother's emotional and mental problems over the span of my lifetime. Only God kept me alive. If Daddy had known what she did to us while he was away he would have sent her to an asylum. Who am I to judge? She obviously doesn't remember doing all those horrid things to us so she must have been quite mad at the time.

Journal Entry

Today is Be Kind to Steve Day since he's out there working hard physical labor to provide for us. I hope he adapts a little better to the work this week. He said he was too old to move furniture. I assume he was thinking of it as a long-term commitment instead of getting through the holidays. I wish the postal service or Motorola would call him.

Lord, You are my provider–not Steve or anyone else. You have always shown up right on time. Please give Steve wisdom, Lord. You know I fear losing the house. Steve said the other day, "Well, that's the only thing left to lose."

As I feel better and better each day, the thought of returning to work entices me. Right now, though, I believe God has given me this time to come to a healing place–to be brought back together again. It will take hours of prayer and meditation. Spending time with Jesus. But then again, with the touch of His hand, He could say "Enough, you've worked hard. Well done. Now get about your Father's business!"

Journal Entry Written by Daphne

I called Dan this morning and talked to him as myself, Daphne. Faith told him about us, so I decided to call him myself. I was afraid to call because I didn't know how he'd respond. I only talked to him for about ten minutes. Maybe less. He and his family are going out of town until the New Year's Eve service. I will miss him.

Now I wish I had gone to church yesterday so I could have gotten a hug. Feel like crying this morning–me and Annie, both. Don't know why, but we're scared because we don't have any money and Steve quit the moving job. I wanted to kick his butt and force him into keeping the job, but Faith says to let him make his own decisions. Hmmm...

Viv just called. Annie came up with her own name for Vivien. She calls her "Vivie." Annie talked to her about the boy wanting to go fishing with Faith. She talked about us sharing time out and sharing Josh's "mama time" when he's home. Vivie encouraged Annie to bake cookies during the day today while the boy was at the center. The Nutcracker was on TV in the background and Annie recognized it. Vivie prayed with Annie about learning to share and about Steve finding a job.

I told Viv about Faith's idea of taking Maymee to an African-American church. It will be an adventure of sorts to find a church with a good music program. I, Daphne, would like to attend the Nutcracker.

We are crying this morning, not sure why, yet. Ate a good breakfast, so it must be issues. I know Annie and I are feeling frightened about Steve not having a job. Faith (or is it Maymee?) always trusts in Jesus to provide–but we aren't quite there yet!

Steve came back and called me "Honey." I'm not his honey, but Faith likes him.
– Daphne

Journal Entry Written by Faith and Daphne

Happy Birthday, Jesus of Nazareth, Son of the living God! It is You we give praise to this Christmas Day because we love You.

Yesterday Daphne cried a couple of times when she thought about Dan leaving town. It triggered her abandonment issues BIG TIME! It also triggered all the other issues of being a preacher's kid. Like thinking everyone was more important to Daddy than me. And when there was time only for quick hugs, quick prayers, quick everything–go, go, go, hurry, hurry–CRASH! Daddy tried. He took us fishing and my brother hunting. He bragged about how other preachers' families were failing, but he took time for his.

Daphne was preoccupied with seeing Dan and getting attention from him before he left. We were courting disaster. Sabotage! She rounded the corner and almost ran into him coming down the hall. He was a man on a mission to do this and that, and then to get out of there. Daphne didn't see it that way. She took his abruptness personally and was very disappointed. His eyes were in that "shut-off" mode. Cold and unfeeling.
– Faith

All I wanted was for him to hug me. A good long hug. And for him to see how upset I was over him leaving town. I wanted him to realize that he was paramount in my world. Faith doesn't understand me. She keeps telling me to grow up.

She started telling me I was crazy to expect from him. That he was in a hurry to be with his wife and family, not me. She was trying to help, but I wish she would keep her nose out of my business!

Well, Dan can go jump in the lake.

Faith says we can't trust any man to meet our needs. What are we doing here, then? I thought he was like a positive father figure.

I can't stand your picking me apart all the time, Faith! The fact is, that he hurt my feelings and I felt pretty raunchy about it. And you weren't there for me either, so buzz off! Maybe you'll hear from me and maybe you won't. I just might take over as the one in front. That would teach you to treat me like crap!
– Daphne

Journal Entry – a.m.

Daphne was dreaming about Dan right before we woke up today. In the dream, she was getting exclusive personal attention from him. I wish she would get over this fixation with him. I'm feeling a little impatient with her. Sometimes it's blurry, the fine line between her and me. Sometimes we're alike. Other times we are distinctly different.

"This is a wonderful Christmas! I got everything I wanted! Thank you for the fly-cast reel and hunting knife!" Josh is beaming.

"Hey, as long as my child has a happy Christmas, then so do I."

Well, I'm not happy! I thought I'd get the baby doll I asked for.

I'm sorry, Annie, I have a gift for you under the tree. Do you like the coloring book and modeling clay I got you?

I guess so, but why didn't Santa bring me a baby doll?

I don't know, dear. Please don't look so sad. I'll get you a baby doll.

"Mom, are you sure you opened all your presents?" Josh says with a mischievous grin.

"Yeah, hon."

"Are you sure you opened *all* of them?"

"What do you mean—hey! That wasn't there before. Ooh, what a beautiful porcelain doll!"

I won't get to play with her. She's not even soft and cuddly. I wanted something I could hug the daylights out of. That doll is too stiff and hard–cold and beautiful. That doll is Daphne!

"Thank you, guys."

"Why are you carrying the doll? We need to go," Steve says as we head out to spend the afternoon with Vivien and her family.

"I want to take her to show Viv."

Upon arriving, I hold the doll up. "Look, Vivien. This is what Steve and Josh gave me for Christmas."

"She's beautiful!"

"I know." Frowning, "Annie asked for a baby doll. She's disappointed in this one."

"Why don't you take our baby Jesus baby doll for Annie."

"Really? Thanks, Vivie." I give her a hug. Baby Jesus is as big as a real baby with a cloth body and floppy arms and legs. I doubt Jesus had yellow hair, though.

"You're welcome. You may keep it as long as you like."

"What's that for?" Steve asks. "We already gave you a doll."

"I know, but Annie wanted a baby doll. The one you gave me is too delicate to love on."

"How are you going to carry them both?"

"It's called multitasking," Vivien's husband quips.

"Ooooh–good one, Stan." I grin. Vivien and I sit at the kitchen table and visit when her two daughters enter.

"Merry Christmas, Jenica and Bryana."

"Merry Christmas, Miss Faith." After hugs all around we exchange the usual Christmas chit-chat about gifts and such.

Changing the subject. "All you kids were very silly in choir last week," I scold with a smile.

"Why? What did they do?" Vivien asks.

"They told me I said something I'm pretty sure I didn't."

"What did they tell you?"

"I had a child recite the rules. When he got to No Talking, he said, 'Zip your lips, lock them up, and throw away the key.' That's silly. When I asked where he got that from the whole group said he got it from me the week before. Of course, I denied it several times, but they kept insisting. I think they were just being silly."

"You did say it," both girls reply in unison.

"I didn't like the idea of not being able to unlock my lips if I threw the key away," Jenica says. "So I pretended to twist a lock like the one on my bedroom door."

"You also had your hair in a bunch of little braids all around your head." Bryana uses both hands to indicate several areas on her head.

"Hmmm...I think I do recall that. I guess I *was* silly that night." I suspect Annie was in front that night.

Journal Entry – p.m.

Went to Stan and Viv's for Christmas dinner. Wow! It was great! I worried about Josh and his level of patience with Viv's four children, but he did very well. Thank You, Lord!

We ate, opened presents, and enjoyed Jesus' birthday party. I wished for more quality time with Viv. I hadn't expected it since I get so easily distracted by all the activity. But I still hoped.

I think I shut down the inside people in order to deal with the noise level. I felt content and must have been able to dissociate enough that the children did not bother me.

This was a pleasant surprise. At the end of the evening, Annie couldn't stand it any longer and had to come out to play on the floor with the kids.

Annie is always with me.

Cooking–umm, eggs, Mama, yummy!

Yes, Annie, it does smell good.

I'm hungry, Mama.

I know. It's almost ready.

Annie is jumping a little bit–clapping her hands and smacking her lips–dancing a jig on her way to the table. I wonder if this is reparenting–allowing her to enjoy the smells and taste of healthful food.

I want more, Mama.

No. We'll have some later.

Okay.

I've noticed I stop and daydream when writing. I know I need to work with Daphne, but I am reluctant to do so.

Think I'll backtrack and finish off that page about Christmas Eve night and how she felt.

Daphne is miffed at me. Feeling misunderstood, she's threatening to come to the front as the presenting person. That simply cannot happen. She will wear me out physically and emotionally. She either sulks and pouts when she's upset or tortures me with threats of inappropriate behavior. She has the power to embarrass me.

Journal Entry – a.m.

Daphne work: I think the line between Daphne and me is very fine. She represents that part of me who still cares what others think about her. She's more concerned with performance than an inner walk with Jesus. Sometimes I am so repelled by all these things I recoil in horror and disdain at her hang-ups.

I am told I must love her. How will I facilitate new behaviors and personality traits if I embrace all these monstrosities? Yet, isn't life-changing growth brought about by facing the ugly and committing to change?

Maybe there's a new level of processing the memory that Daphne brought. Maybe that will help her grow up and come closer to where I am on all this recovery work. What does the "inner work" have in store for me? I've enjoyed this reprieve from the extreme mental and emotional pain.

Thank You, Jesus! You are my life! Please continue to breathe Your healing through my system. Please shine Your light on anything You need me to face. I love You, Jesus.

Journal Entry – p.m.

I've begun an almost continuous conversation reassuring Annie, loving her, and parenting her. She's been a link to my overeating. When I take care of her and she doesn't feel deprived she's content with my "grown-up" decisions. It's truly amazing how it works.

Daphne is obsessed with Dan. She thinks of him constantly. What would he think of this? How would he respond to that? I've been able to notice how preoccupied she is with winning his approval. She never won it with the daddy.

My ears felt funny–almost split away from my body while writing this.

Daphne's existence depends on what the daddy thinks, how he responds, and whether he loves her. She pushes everyone and herself to the max to "do" and "be" that perfect princess Daddy wanted her to be. Being his daughter gave her power and clout in her world and she learned to rule as cunningly as he.

He could turn her emotions with a nod of the head or a certain look in his eyes. Those cold, clear piercing blue eyes looked straight through her. Why didn't she have eyes like his? She was stuck with brown eyes, like the mother's. Nobody liked the mother.

He rewarded her with public praise and held her up for all to see.
She couldn't breathe. She couldn't be.
She was his puppet. His prize. His pawn.
He played her well.

He made her who she is today–this Daphne.
– Faith

Journal Entry by Faith and Daphne

Had a session with Dr. Kathy and caught her up on all we've been doing. Young Daphne got in touch with her pain about the sexual abuse. She cried and vented a lot then became angry, finally getting in touch with her anger towards Daddy. She wished she had bit him, fought him. She was just a little girl.
– Faith

My daddy did nasty things to me. I was a good girl. Why did he do that to me? I did everything he wanted to please him. I wanted him to be happy with me! I was only a little girl. My body was sweet and soft, innocent and pure until he touched me. It felt good. I craved his affection. But then it felt wrong, like I was a bad girl. Like it was my fault it happened

He said I was a good girl and was kind to me when I sang pretty. I could tell it made him look like a good man. Faith says I was his puppet. Maybe she's right. Why do I hurt so much when all I did was please him?

Faith threw his t-shirts away. She didn't want them anymore.
– Daphne

1997

Journal Entry – a.m.

I'll go where You want me to go, dear Lord. Thank You, Jesus, for a new year, and thank You for sending Gini to visit. Got a lot of Gini love. I cried with her. Feeling pretty vulnerable and weepy today.

Earlier today, on the way to Viv's to borrow her muffin pans, Annie had an anxiety attack. She got lost and had not eaten breakfast and was hungry. We cried all the way to Viv's house. Guess this was going to be a weepy sort of day.

Thank You for Vivien, Lord! She fed me oatmeal and gave me hugs and let me cry. I could never get enough hugs, especially when I'm Annie.

Lying down to journal is not always a good idea. I fell asleep. I started this day off crying. Now I'm ending it crying. Jesus, please hold me!

I want some time with Dan but I'm aware of how valuable his time is. Is this me or Daphne? If it's Daphne, that's good, because she's beginning to think of someone other than herself for a change! I don't know. Sometimes she's so quiet when I look inside. Could it be that she has come to the front and that's why I don't see her because she's not in there but out here? Interesting thought. That could be it, or she's turned away from me, choosing to be silent for whatever reasons. Jesus, help me reach Daphne.

Journal Entry – p.m.

I dreamed I kept trying to get to Daddy's church in time to play the piano for service but was late. The first song started already with Mother playing the organ alone. Scrambling to get to the piano during the song, I tried to find the page number, etc. The dream was repeated two or three times. I finally gave up and didn't even go to church at all.

Another dream: Stuffy people visited my mother's house. Mother was doing her hair to go to church early for a pre-service meeting. She told me she has to go because, after all, she's the president. I wrote on her mirror with a lipstick sample, "I want you Mommy." When she entered the room the lipstick had vanished like disappearing ink.

A difficult day, laughing and crying. Annie and little Daphne are very needy. Pain is unbearable. Waves of emotions well up and I cry and cry.

Journal Entry

Waking up crying. I dreamed a lot last night. I may recall some later. I couldn't sleep at three a.m. I'm so tired. I lay there holding the baby doll and crying, praying to Jesus to hold me.

I called Dan when I got up at 8:30. I prayed about calling him and felt okay about it so I did. I asked him to pray with me. He asked how it was going. I told him hard. He asked about Annie, Daphne, and Maymee. He asked if it usually helped when I saw Dr. Kathy. I told him yes.

Thank You, Lord, he is trying to understand. He was so gracious to listen and pray with me. Give him a big hug for me.

Maymee is excited about singing in the Martin Luther King Day Mass Choir! We're trying to figure out what to do with Daphne during that time. Would like to let Maymee sing in Bethesda's choir, too.

Maybe we could put Daphne to sleep in her little cottage by the sea. Make it so she can't hear, see, or feel the performance issues that come up when she is co-conscious. Can we request her to be way in the back in the subconscious or whatever you call it? Don't want to jeopardize her recovery though. I need to do what's best for her. I'm sure Maymee won't mind waiting for another opportunity.

I know you want to sing, Maymee. You've been there so much for me, girl. Thank you. That's why the mass choir might be something you could do cuz nobody would know you there.

If only Daddy knew about you, Maymee. Wouldn't we have had some fun getting back at him!! HA! Maybe he'll flip over in his grave.

Anger is supposed to be good. It hurts. But if each alter can process the anger of each abusive situation, healing comes quickly. Right?

Maymee Calls Vivien

♪ When Will This Valley Bloom ♪

When I wake up each morning, I feel like crying,
And the pain inside is so heavy, I feel like dying.
Questions come. Why, Lord?
What do you have planned for me?
All I want to know is that You have me
In Your nail-scarred hands.

When will this valley begin to bloom?
How long must I stay inside this room?
The pain is so deep, it's hard to sleep,
Please let me know that somehow You're in control,
Please let me know that Jesus, You're in control.

Maybe one day when I awake, the sun'll be shining
And the pain that I've been feeling will be subsiding.
Who knows if my questions will be answered by then?
All I want to know is He's holding me
In His nail-scarred hands.

But as many as received Him,
to them He gave the the right to become children of God,
to those who believe in His name, who were born,
not of blood, nor of the will of the flesh,
nor the will of a man, but of God.

John 1:12,13 (NASB)

Behold what manner of love
the Father has bestowed on us,
that we should be called children of God!

1 John 3:1a (NASB)

1997

Journal Entry Written by Faith and Maymee

Went to group. Sent Daphne to a quiet place so Maymee could go to church and sing in the choir. Oh yeah!

Maymee is now at the front to give me a rest. She got up and got dressed this morning and went to group. Only one outfit in the closet would do for her today. Yikes!

Maymee sang a "Holy is the Lord" medley at group and was thrilled to get to sing about Jesus! I told the group about the MLK Day mass choir and they were very supportive and excited for us.

Feel like playing "hooky" from the pain. Maymee told Dr. Kathy that Baby Girl (Faith) needed a rest and the two little baby cakes (Annie and Daphne) needed time off from the pain.
– Faith

I think they've hurt enough this week. I'm concerned about our body an' how tired it's made Baby Girl goin' through these last several days. It's so great to be in front. To get to be me. Get to choose my clothin', etc.

One thing I'm concerned about–really it's one of my pet peeves–is we have no decent clothes. For whatever reason, many personal things have been neglected. Now, I know there hasn't been much money, but we need our dignity, too.

She's promised to take us shoppin' at a resale shop. Dear Jesus, please let some nice clothes be there. Clothes that fit the budget, but we'll all feel good wearin.' And shoes. Oh, dear Father in Heaven, we need some shoes. Where to start? And with so few resources. Maybe we'll be able to get some work before long.

Today when Baby Girl asked me to come to the front–it was so good to be able to do that. This time there were tears of joy! I'm so excited about havin' figured out a way to be in the choir at Bethesda. I must guard my stress level, even happy stress. Thank You, Jesus! Don't want to cycle too far into hypomania. Jesus, hold my hand!

I surprised myself on the way to group. I glanced in the mirror an' saw a white girl lookin' back at me! Dr. Kathy said that was typical. Well, black is beautiful–that's all there is to it! An' her hair! Oh, good Lord! Cain't do nothin' with her hair, but we'll manage.

Thank You, Jesus. Heal us, Jesus. You are the only One who can!
– Maymee

Journal Entry Written by Maymee

It worked! We put Daphne in the back of the system–an' young Daphne and Annie with angels–to give 'em a break from the pain. It's been great to be the one in the front.

Whew, honey, I cain't wait to see the day when all our inner turmoil will be no more. When Baby Girl'll be all right. Dawlin', just remember Jesus is not gonna let go of you. He's got a hold of you, baby. That's stronger than that there bulldog's bite when he's a holdin' on.

He is able! He can do it. Yes, He can. He's been there all this time–listenin' an' He ain't goin' nowhere! Thank You, Lord Jesus. Whew. Hallelujah!

Take it all to Him, honey. When you're wantin' to give up, Baby Girl. You think I don't remember 'bout the time your mother hit you upside the head with that pipe? Girl, Jesus was there an' He prevented you from gettin' a concussion! An' that time she almost drowned you in the kitchen sink. God saved you then, too.

He gave you that gift to split off outta the pain, honey. You know, dawlin', that's where Maymee comes from. From you. When she slapped you. When she tried to drown you. When she kept tellin' you she was gonna get you a black mama. So I was your mama. Ha! We fixed her!

I took all that stuff for you. Jesus did too. Oh dawlin', He loves you. Jesus loves you, Nathan, an' Joey. Why, He even loves that ole Hitler in that prison. And Annie, Jesus loves Annie, too. You hear me little babycakes?

Baby, my people were taught-no honey-they weren't taught, they were forced to endure the hardship of slavery. You don't know it, girl, but you can endure too. You're a lot tougher than you think. I'm a part of you, honey, and that's tougher than shoe leather!

So get that lip off the ground. Put on some glory music an' chase that ole devil right outta here, Baby Girl. Yes! In the name of Jesus.
- Maymee

Love that Maymee!

Journal Entry - Written by Maymee

> The Lord is my light and my salvation-whom I shall fear? The Lord is the stronghold of my life-of whom shall I be afraid.
> - Psalm 27:1 (NIV)

Thank You, Father, for showing up. I don't mean that disrespectfully either like You never show up or something 'cause, praise You, Jesus, You're always there. Always here for me!

Thank You for Christian radio. I love how they sing about You, Jesus. Always about You! You're the One! That's all it's about, Father. In the shadow of Your wings-that's where I want to be today, Lord. Please hold me. I'm so weary.

Today I daydreamed about how my "spirit," the real me looked. It's certainly different than this body I now reside in. I'm thin and graceful with long ballerina legs. I can dance effortlessly without a song. The song is in my heart and my mind. The music is always there, a never-ending symphony of love for life.

My energy is endless and I dance everywhere I go. The song tickles my toes and limbs as I allow them to express the beauty of the melody. Everyone I touch is filled with awe and wonder at the creation of God in my soul. I give to needy helpless creatures who wander across my path.

I'm dancin' to the next movement with purpose and intensity. I know why I am created so I dance-touchin' others with God's love. There is no loss of sleep over this ethereal body. No painful memories. Only the dance. I know I must dance. When I don't dance, I sing of the One whom I adore. The One whose creation I am. I sing. I dance. I touch. Then I awake from my daydream. If only they knew what I really looked like. Who I really am. What I can really do.
– Maymee

"Hi, Viv. How are ya, girl frayend?" I settle down in my comfy chair with the phone in hand.

"Hi, Faith. I'm fine. How are you?"

"I'm Maymee. Baby Girl, Daphne, an' Annie needed some relief from the pain, so Dr. Kathy suggested we send Annie and Faith to stay with Daphne in her safe house and I come out front for a while."

"Okaaay..." This is the first time I've talked to Viv. I hear a brief touch of apprehension in her voice, but she soon sounds relaxed.

"Daphne wrote something in the journal the other day. Would you like to hear it?"

"Sure."

"Let me get it." I fetch it from the bedroom and return to my comfy chair. "Here it is. 'My daddy did nasty things to me. I was a good girl. Why did he do that to me? I did everything he wanted to please him. I wanted him to be happy with me! I was only a little girl…'"

"Wow. That makes me so sad. Can I pray with you?"

"Yes, please."

"Father in heaven, I praise Your holy name. Father, thank You for loving Faith, Annie, Maymee, and Daphne. Lord, I lift little Daphne up to You and ask You to hold her in Your arms. Let her feel Your love. Let her see Your face and know You love her just the way she is.

"Father, please take away Daphne's shame. Assure her that the blood of Jesus can make her clean and whole. Make her a new creation, the way she was before she was defiled. Cover her with Your presence and Your love. Let her see herself clothed in Christ radiating heavenly light as bright as Your Son. Transform her into a new, pure, clean, and innocent creation in You. Fill her with Your joy. Overflowing abundantly with great, great joy. I ask it in the name of Jesus, amen."

"Swew! Thank you, Viv. Thank You, Jesus!…Wow! I see little Daphne. She's regressin' to a baby in diapers, probably around one and a half to two years old. Jesus just walked in! Oh hallelujah, the great waves of joy! He's scoopin' her up and is proppin' her on His lap–you know–like we've all done with our children.

"She senses how much He loves her and has no fear of Him leaving her. The nursery is becomin' very bright as the light of God shines brighter and brighter! He's a cooin' and a coochy-gooin' her and kissin' her fat little toes. He's re-parentin' her. What a revelation! We don't have to reparent her, Jesus does! And He's doin' it right now! He's hummin' to her and mimickin' her noises. She feels completely loved by Him."

"That's exciting! How wonderful! I'll bet He'll take her home with Him," Viv exclaims.

"I'm gonna go journal now."

"Okay. I'll talk to you later."

Journal Entry

Each time we enter the nursery with Jesus and baby Daphne, waves of joy keep coming. It feels so good joyful tears keep falling! Thank You, Jesus!

And now we look to Jesus holding older Daphne in the next room. She stares vacantly as He stands behind her, holding her shoulder. And as we prayed earlier we know the Holy Spirit will know what to do with this older girl. Now that we've prayed, our work is done. We'll just step back and watch what happens as He does His healing work in her.

He is walking from the nursery into the music room, now holding baby Daphne for older Daphne to see. Somehow He wants to reach her through the baby. It's hard for her not to smile at this little gurgler.

Daphne, this is you as a baby. Aren't you adorable? What do you notice about this baby?

She doesn't know anything?

Yes, she's completely innocent. What else?

She's happy?

You're right. She has no worries.

But babies can't worry.

Of course, they can't. Jesus smiles. They have to learn how to worry.

What does she have to do with me?

She is you, only younger, before all the bad stuff.

Yeah, right. Okay.

I want to show you not only can I restore your purity, but I can also restore your mind. The way you think about things.

What's wrong with the way I feel? I mean, what's wrong with the way I think?

Exactly. Daphne, I love you for you. The way I love this baby girl.

Yes, but she's never done anything wrong.

True, and I love her.

And she's never done anything good.

Now you're catching on, Daphne. As My child, I love You! You don't have to play a note, sing a song, or submit to any ugly things for Me to love you.

How so?

I am God. I am love. My love is overwhelming, unconditional, pure God-love. No one can buy it with effort, words, riches, or manipulation. Come, let Me love you, Daphne, simply because you are you.

Because I am me? But I don't know who that is!

I do and I love you.

But I'm not very good. I'm selfish. I'm depressed a lot. I'm stubborn.

My love is more stubborn than you.

That can't be. No one's ever really loved me.

Daphne, sweetheart, *gently taking her chin in His hand,* look into My eyes.

Fearfully, her eyes slowly rise to meet His. She looks at love for the first time, pouring out from His eyes. Shining from His face.

I can't do this. Turning away. I can't stand it.

It's okay. I won't give you more love than you need.

More than I need? She gasps. I've always felt I couldn't get enough. You're saying You have so much love that You won't give me more than I can handle? She's overwhelmed. She becomes shy in His presence.

He stands, waiting for her to let this settle into her heart. She glances up at Him. Love, steady love pouring from Him.

Is it really true? All I need is You?

Yes, it's true. He holds out His hand.

What do you want me to do?

Accept My love.

Will it burn?

No, my child. You will never be burned by the fire of perverted love again.

I don't know how to do this.

I will help you.

I can sing for You or would You like a piano solo? Never really excelled, but I sure tried. Are You hungry? I can make a pie. I don't know what to do.

He stops her and says it again. *You don't have to do anything. I love you, Daphne.*

I can't live this way.

Of course, you can't. That's why you'll need to lean on Me.

Yeah?

Yes. I will tell you every step to take.

Really?

She has regressed to about four years old and stands on top of Jesus' feet while holding His hands. He takes a few steps and they laugh.

Like this?

Yes, exactly. Only I will be the One holding you.

She is teenage Daphne again. She gazes at Him as though trying to discern a difficult mathematical equation. It's so simple and yet so profound.

You will hold me? She gives up trying to figure Him out.

Of course. He sits beside a large picture window. It is growing dark outside. Jesus holds baby Daphne as she sleeps soundly, secure in His love. Older Daphne climbs onto His knee. She's surprised to find out He is big enough to hold her, even though she's mostly grown.

I love you, Daphne, He whispers.

There's so much ugliness inside I don't deserve You. Your love can't be for me!

I paid for all the ugliness and sin, Daphne. I can make you as pure as this sleeping baby. My blood paid for all the sins, all the wrongs. There is a better way to live.

What if I slip and fall?

I'll pick you up.

What if I forget and act like I used to?

I won't stop loving you, Daphne, even if you mess up.

Why am I like this? The baby had no problem trusting You. I want to trust You. After all, what have I got to lose?

I can do the same for you, Daphne. Think it over, okay?

Okay. She sighs and leans her head back against Him. He gently rocks them both and sings them a lullaby. He catches her tears flowing down her cheeks and gently kisses her on the top of her head. She reaches up, hugs Him, then falls asleep.

He looks outside the window into the garden and says, *That's the rose I will pick for her when she awakens.*

Wow! What a God! He's wooin' us! I woulda never guessed that direction in a million years. I gotta share it with Viv.

We praise You, God! There ain't enough words. The human language is too limited to describe You. Wow! Thank You for providin' spiritual guidance. Oh, what an awesome God You are! Know what? You're beautiful! Love Ya, love Ya, love Ya!
– Maymee

Lord, can I share this with Dan? Please guide me, I'm so excited about Your love I can't even think straight. I guess

I'll call him. The worst he can say is he's not available and maybe we can set up an appointment with him so I can read it to him. Tears of joy! I love You, Jesus.

Shared with Steve when he came home! He said he wished he could hear from God, too. He was happy for Daphne. Steve has difficulty dealing with the fact that the Spirit of God is communicating with me. He wants to hear from God himself and is angry that God would communicate with me and not him.

My spirit is wounded when I can't share everything the Spirit tells me with Steve because I love him so much and we're best friends. We've been through hell and back more than once and it's strengthened our relationship. (Take that, Satan!) It hurts when I can't share the intimate relationship I have with Jesus with the one I also love. In due time. God is in control. He has a wonderful plan for us.
– Faith

Journal Entry – a.m.

What do I need today for our special time together this morning, Father?

You need Me.

Right. I just need You. Love Ya, love Ya, love Ya, Lord.

Can't wait for Jesus and Daphne time to see what You have planned, Jesus. You really blessed our socks off yesterday, my Master, my Lord, my King. You alone are worthy to be praised, Jesus. You're the Man! Nobody else but You are all that, Jesus. They might think so, but they're wrong! You're the only One!

I love You today, Lord. I hug You today, Jesus. Lots and lots of hugs to You today, Father. Take my life today, Jesus, and do with it what You will. You are the only One who can make sense of it. Please let me do all to glorify You.

Father, several outside things are competing for my attention today. Some ministry, some personal needs, and some business. Please, Lord, let me walk with You so close I can hear You whisper my name.

Wow! You touched me, Father! I am reluctant to change the pattern we've had of quiet, lovin' Jesus days. The time You've drawn me aside for healing the inner people for loving each other has been so precious! Oh, Jesus, You are so beautiful!

Daphne stirs as she wakes up, still on Jesus' lap. He gives her a hug and motions toward the child still sleeping snuggly in His other arm. They both smile down at the toddler. She is growing. She is growing up in His love.

I want to grow in You, too, Jesus. Please show me how.

He takes her hand. *I love you.*

I'm not sure how to love. I know I can't love like You.

Let me do it for you.

Say what?

Daphne, you don't have to do anything. Let Me do it all for you.

I know. I'm being stubborn, but come on, surely I'm supposed to do something.

Enough time for that later. Now I want to show you how to be in Me and simply enjoy Me.

She is speechless and turns to gaze out the window into the garden. A wave of love causes her to look back into those ever-true, ever-loving eyes. Light is dawning inside her heart like nothing she's ever experienced before.

I want to love Him. He's too good to be true. And I think I believe Him, but how? He stands quietly beside her, in no rush, loving her with His Spirit–waiting.

Finally, she says, *I must tell You that I am unclean. I'm used goods, yesterday's rubbish–defective.*

She slowly reaches into a pocket and pulls out two pieces of a photograph. The small corner remnant is the only part she can bear to see. She timidly shows them to Jesus as He looks over her shoulder. *How can You even look at me, much less love me when You see this?* Instantly, the images fade and the paper vanishes.

Jesus gently touches her on the shoulders, turning her around. *For you, to show you I love you.* In His hand is the loveliest rose she's ever seen. The fragrance sweeps lightly through the room. Oh, what love! The glimmer in her heart flickers a little brighter as she smiles her thanks to Him.

He really does love me. The truth finally begins to tear down the barricade around her heart. *He cares about me!* His Spirit bears witness with hers that she begins to receive and accept His love.

He takes her in His arms and begins to dance with her. She closes her eyes. The brightness of His love fills her being and radiates farther than she could see or imagine.

Then she hears it. The most beautiful melody, the sweetest chords. He is playing His love song to her. *This is our song,* He whispers into her ear. All her barriers vanish at that instant. She falls at His feet, kissing them through her tears.

Forgive me, oh my Jesus. Forgive me, my Love.

The melody plays on. The Father above smiles as He watches Jesus, His Son, loving this little child, Daphne. The Spirit smiles because she has finally let Him in! They each continue to dance to the melody Jesus wrote for her.

"Hi, Viv. Isn't God good? I just called to fill you in on all the latest. I'm so grateful for the miracle God gave me with Daphne, I'm anxious to see who He's going to work with next."

"Are you sure He's finished with Daphne? Why don't you ask the Holy Spirit if He's finished with her? I don't know why, but I envision Daphne with fetters and chains of unforgiveness on her arms and legs."

"Well, let's ask Him. Thank You, Jesus, for the love You're showing Daphne. Thank You for finally breaking down the barriers around her heart so she can love You. Thank You for wooing her. Father, I'd like to know if You're finished with Daphne or not. Please reveal anything we need to work on with You. In Jesus' name, amen."

"Faith, I suspect Daphne won't be whole until she forgives her offenders. That may include herself and/or God. I see each link in the chain binding her as a person and event that Daphne needs to forgive. You may want to ask the Lord to see if I'm perceiving correctly."

"Let's pray again, then. Father, we give everything to You. Holy Spirit, please take over Your work and continue as only You can. I'm listening. I'm willing to submit to Your will. If You want to work in dreams during rest time, please provide the time for recording Your work."

"You need to make time for God to work on the inside people every day, despite distractions."

Journal Entry – p.m.

Faith, pick up the baby doll, Jesus says. My heart feels heavy as I lift the doll.

Take it to the rocking chair. I begin to rock and cuddle the baby.

Look at the baby. I'm holding it out in front of me. *It's your daddy.*

Wow! Yes, everyone has to be a baby sometime. Even You chose to be a baby. Looking at the doll, I picture it as my daddy. Holding it close to my breast, I rock him, wondering how my grandmother may have felt as she rocked him.

Waiting for more from the Lord. Feeling sleepy, I lean my head back and doze. BANG! The baby doll falling to the wooden floor awakens me.

You are to forgive your ancestors first because it was they who dropped the baby, Jesus tells me.

So this is the first link to the chain, to forgive my ancestors. I don't even have to know the details of how or why they dropped the baby. I need to forgive them for doing so. Drawing the baby close I rock it for a while.

This is how I wish your daddy had been loved. I want to love all My children with this kind of tenderness.

Sometimes there are no words or thoughts when God reveals such wonders. I sit quietly rocking, mulling over all

He's revealing. Somehow, someone or something in Daddy's upbringing wounded him and caused him to become spiritually lame.

Wow! What a God!

Fatigue sweeps in. *May I take a nap?*

Yes, but not too long. I have work for you to do.

The ringing of the telephone shatters my restful sleep. I jump up and the baby doll falls off the bed, reminding me of what God was telling me. My ancestors. Somebody dropped the baby. I must forgive them for this.

Choir is special tonight. Dan is super busy and can't meet with me right now. His secretary is very sweet about it–he's not available.

God is so great. The timing of His healing with Daphne is so incredible! A week ago she would have been extremely hurt, crying and stamping her feet to get her way. But with her eyes on Jesus instead of Dan–or Daddy–she is so much at peace!

Wow! Jesus, You are so good! The rejection she normally would feel is nonexistent now. Praise Your name, Lord! You are my God, I am Your servant!

Regrettably, I cannot share with Dan, though. I think he'd be blessed. Think I'll write to him and let him off the hook for a response. God, bless Dan today. Bless his work for You.

A Banquet for Annie

God Almighty

To write the notes of my soul
Blends deep within my spirit.
And He is there.

To write my daily thoughts and qualms
Celebrates the essence of my life.
He is my life.

To write love sonnets to my Lord
Flushes my cheeks with joy.
He is my king.

To write praises in His honor
Frees my voice to sing.
He is my song.

To write and write and write some more
Fills my life with meaning.
He is my God.

> Let Him lead me to the banquet hall,
> and let His banner over me be love.
> Strengthen me with raisins,
> refresh me with apples,
> for I am faint with love.
>
> Song of Solomon 2:4,5 (NASB)

1997

"Hello?"

"Hi, Faith. How's everything going?"

"Great, Viv. Been spending a lot of time with Annie. I'm helping her learn to make healthful choices in her diet."

"Would you like me to pray for Annie?"

"Sure!"

"Father, I praise Your holy name and thank You for the wonderful work You're doing in Daphne and Faith. Father, I pray for Your richest blessings to pour out on Annie. Please invite Annie to Your banquet table. Show her all the wonderful food You have laid out. Then let her eat. Let her eat all she desires until she has had enough. Let her know Yours is the food she needs. Not contaminated earthly food, but pure nourishing food from Your table. Fill her with Your Bread of Life and the fruit of Your Holy Spirit. Cause her to spit out seeds of discontentment. Most of all, fill her with Your love. In Jesus' name, amen."

Journal Entry

Wow! Lord, Your ways are wonderful.

I haven't felt as split since the miracle with Daphne. Feel like Faith instead of Maymee, even. Are you leaving Maymee around to be strong in You, Lord, or do You have other things planned? I enjoy the part of me that is Maymee. Lord, please let me hang onto her boldness.

So, You are inviting Annie to Your banquet table in this new House of Love You made for her. Annie accepts. Together we approach the banquet room...

Will you take me, Mama?

Yes, Annie, I'll go with you.

What's He like?

He's very nice. You will like Him. He's making a banquet for you. Do you know what a banquet is,?

No.

It's a great big feast with bunches and bunches of food!

Wowee!

Yes! Wowee!

Giggling. *Mama?*

Humm?

Will there be other kids there, too?

Not this time. This party is just for you.

For me? Why?

Because He loves you.

Why?

He loves everybody in the whole wide world. Are you ready?

Sticking her hand in her mouth, she nods her head. We approach immense double doors. I reach up to knock but Jesus appears, welcoming us into His presence. Annie hides behind me and peeks out at Him.

Jesus gets down on His knees to her level. *Hi Annie! Thank you for coming today. Do you like parties?*

Yes! Clapping her hands with glee. *I'm hungry, Mama. I'm hungry, Jesus.*

Pausing before the elaborate doorway. *Get ready, Annie!*

Jesus throws the doors open wide. The sight before us is incredible. A very long table stands in the center of the room. A white tablecloth reaches the floor. The table is adorned with a breathtaking rainbow of colors. Yellow, orange, and red fruits and vegetables in glass bowls. Cheeses and various meats surround floral centerpieces.

And desserts! Oh, the desserts! Three-tiered cakes with pastel flowers cascading around the sides. Chocolate cupcakes with fancy swirling sprinkle-covered frosting. Fruit pies covered with decorative crust cutouts. Large bowls filled with a rainbow of sherbet, ice cream, and whipped cream. This, and so much more.

Annie gasps at the sight of it! She clutches my hand. Jesus allows her to survey in wide-eyed wonder. She meanders around the full length of the table in silent awe at the bounty. She comes to a solitary place setting of floral china and shiny silver flatware. A small silver stand displays a card with her name.

Look, Mama, my name!

Yes, Annie, this is your place at the table.

Annie begins to weep, overcome with the thought of so much food.

Are you hungry, Annie? Jesus asks. She nods her head. *What would you like first?*

Annie chooses an enticing dessert topped with a rippling mound of whipped cream. She glances at me, expecting disapproval. She and I are learning to eat foods that are good for us.

I nod. It's okay this time.

She looks around the perimeters of the room as though searching for something. Jesus assures her, *Annie, there are no closets in this house. This is My House of Love.*

No closets?

Not even one.

What about people?

Only Me and Daphne. Do you know Daphne?

Yes! She is my friend.

Well then, you see, no one will hurt you here. You are safe here.

Her eyes hungrily devour the vast white room and the coveted food but says, *Can I go play now?*

Aren't you hungry?

If I eat, won't You get mad?

No, Annie. He lifts the cover off a large platter to display a neatly stacked pile of hamburgers. *This food is for you.*

Wow! I like hamburgers!

I know you do! Go ahead. Eat up.

Lifting one, she begins to chow down. *Yum!*

Eat all you want.

All I want?

Yes, all you want.

But I want it ALL!

And I want to give it to you.

You do?

Can I tell you a secret?

I don't like secrets.

Well, this is a fun one. We'll tell Mama too, okay?

Okay.

This food is not like the food you and Mama eat.

It's not?

No, it's not. This food will last forever and ever.

You mean I'm gonna be great big and fat and stay that way forever? Woah!

No, no, no. When you eat this food, you will be taking in my love with every bite.

Huh? Why?

Because I love you, Annie.

Silly. Of course, You do.

But I want to love you better than anybody's ever loved you.

Why?

Because I am Jesus Christ of Nazareth, the Son of the living God. I want to help you be all better.

It hurts.

I know.

When I do eat, it hurts, and when I don't eat, it still hurts.

I know.

Either way, it feels bad.

Not a good way to feel, huh? Know what?

What?

I'm not going to punish you for eating.

No?

No. Nor will I punish you for NOT eating.

Not at all?

Even if you don't eat at this party. Either way will be fine with Me.

She tests Him by filling her plate high with all manner of food. She begins to eat, taking occasional furtive looks at Him. After a while, she decides happiness is getting to eat all you want of your favorite foods without getting into trouble. Annie is the happiest little girl in the whole-wide-world!

Forgiving

Darling, Darling Daphne

"Darling, Darling Daphne,
You were made to dance in sunlight.
You were made to sing out loud.
You are beautiful. You are lovely.
You are everything," he vowed.
In starlight how you glimmered.

Now the darkness and harsh reality have come.
All your glitter, little firefly, has gone.
When you look into the mirror
of your ever-aching heart,
Oh, the ugly, dirty, rotten figure
of a face falling apart.
See the wicked downright hateful.
Don't stop looking. That's a start.

Run away. Oh, run, run forever.
But there's no place to hide.
Dim highways and now corridors,
the hallways of your mind.
It's not over. You can't end it.
Life is there for you to live.
Daddy's gone, and you're forgiven
now it's your turn to forgive.

Giving love and giving life
is not an easy thing for you.
Take my hand, hold it tight,
and I'll show you what to do.
We must walk this road together,
for we shall never part.
I must love you. You must listen.
I'm crying from my heart.
I don't know all the answers.
My mind's an open vat.
But together we will find them.
You can be very sure of that.

There's a God up in heaven
who looks nothing like my dad.
He knows all that has happened
and He doesn't think we're bad.
When we struggle–and we *will* struggle
On this newly laid out road,
He'll protect us and will guide us.
And on that, you've got my word.

Now I rejoice, not that you were made sorry,
but that your sorrow led to repentance.
For you were made sorry in a godly manner,
that you might suffer loss from us in nothing.
For godly sorrow produces repentance
leading to salvation, not to be regretted;
but the sorrow of the world produces death.

1 Corinthians 7:9,10 (NKJV)

1997

Journal Entry

ATTACK! I come against the fear of rejection in the name of Jesus Christ of Nazareth! Fear has nagged at me since several people haven't returned my calls. I feel people are holding me off at arm's length for some reason.

This could be paranoia and a genuine attack of the enemy because of recent victories. Lord, I'm open to You shining a light on me to show me where I might be turning people off. Is it because I get so excited when You're working in me? Do I need a quieter spirit? Is this the issue You want to work on in me right now or am I becoming sidetracked from the work You want to do with Annie?

Go to the piano.

Already, my spirit is quieting and soothing my fears as I play. I'm focusing back on You. In the presence of Jehovah, God Almighty, Prince of Peace.

Back in Your presence...

Forgive me, Lord, for once again looking to man for approval and my self-worth. How could I do this when You love me so much and so recently showed me Your amazing love?

I forgive you, Daphne.

You knew I'd fall, didn't You?

Yes, but I was ready to catch you because you are willing to let Me be Lord.

Oh, Jesus, You are the only One I can trust. I can't even trust myself. But You are true, steady love. Thank You, Jesus, for not being a fantasy, but the living Son of God. I do get over-excited about things. I'm so impatient! I'm sorry I'm so needy.

I love you and accept You, Daphne.

I need You so much!

Yes you do, and I'm right here!

I wish I were more like You.

We're working on it.

Thank You, Jesus! You are the One to keep me on track. How much love You have shown me through Your work with Daphne. Father, what next? More work on Daphne? Back to Annie? You know what's best.

"Hi, Viv! I just had to call and tell you everything God is doing in me today. Annie ate hamburgers at Jesus' banquet table. She's with Him now."

"Hamburgers, huh? I would have thought for sure it would be lamb or roast or something more nutritious."

"She had a dessert covered with whipped topping before that!"

"Hmmm."

"God is doing so much with Annie and Daphne. I thought we were making some serious headway until I got an attack of fear today. I feel like people were avoiding me. How can I still be so messed up when He's doing so much?"

"It sounds like God isn't finished with Daphne, yet. It's more like He's just begun."

"I feel so naïve to think she was all taken care of since His recent work with her. I was under the impression it would be quick work. My coming together to be one, especially since He's been doing so much work in me!"

"I imagine you sitting in a wagon on the top of a mountain, just ready to fly down."

Itttsss sssoo cccold! I'm ffffrrreezzzing! Steve is warm, why am I so very cold?

Prostitutes?! Where did they come from? I come against the spirit of Jezebel in the name of Jesus! Just a bad dream.

Not JUST a dream. You need to pay more attention to your husband in public and less attention to other men.

Yes, Lord. Steve needs the extra loving anyway.

Journal Entry – a.m.

Lord, I feel insane today. I know it's like what a friend and I spoke of yesterday. What is reality here on this plane is a totally different reality on a spiritual plane. Can I buy a ticket for the spiritual plane?

> Remember Your word to Your servant, for You have given me hope. My comfort in my suffering is this; Your promise preserved my life.
> – Psalm 119: 49,50 (NIV)

"Hi, Viv. Would you please pray with me? I feel like there are entities God wants to cleanse out of my system."

"Sure. Father, I know it's Your will that Faith be cleansed of any demonic oppression. So we ask You in the name of Jesus to cleanse her now. We come against fear, worry, oppression, and profanity in the name of Jesus and tell you to leave our presence, NOW."

"Whatever is in the holding cell, I'm telling you to go in the name of Jesus and never come back."

"...And don't come to my house either!" Vivien commands.

"Father put angels around Viv's house and protect her family from Satan's attack for helping me. Amen."

"Faith, I think Daphne is going to have to go through a cleansing fire as she faces her abuse and begins to forgive."

"Oh no. I'm not sure she can do that. Memories alone are terrifying! I'm not sure I'm up to it."

"It will be very different this time. Like Shadrach, Meshach, and Abednego in the fiery furnace, the Son of the living God will be with Daphne. Not a hair on her head will be singed, nor will she, or her clothing even smell of smoke. The pain she will experience will be of the 'That-hurts-so-GOOD' kind."

"Come again?"

"Did I tell you about my friend, Paul?"

"I don't think so."

"He's working on a degree in counseling and mentors me from time to time. After I prayed with young Daphne and you had your first visitation from Jesus I called Paul. He's given me tips on how to help you.

"Anyway, he once told me he smashed his thumbnail. It turned black and was extremely painful. Instead of getting better, it got progressively worse. His whole thumb was red and swollen, so he went to the doctor. The doctor drilled a small hole in the nail, relieving the pressure of the blood under the nail. I'll spare you the graphic details, but Paul said although it hurt like mad, the release hurt so good! Only because he submitted to painful treatment was his thumb able to heal."

"Necessary pain, huh?"

"I'm afraid so."

"*You're* afraid?"

"The only way to emotional freedom is to scrutinize each memory and deal with it. Would you like to pray God will provide a way for me to assist Daphne through her journey?"

"You bet I would."

"Okay, let's do it."

Journal Entry

Josh is nearly a teenager now. Been having serious problems with him. Had to place him in a boys' home. It's making a big difference. We're reviewing principles on boundaries and respect. He showed up for a surprise visit today! Funny, it didn't even enter my mind that he'd be coming home today. Counselors brought him.

I wonder who mothers this child.

"Hi, Viv. Come on in. Josh's watching TV in the den, so we can pray in the living room. Would you like anything to drink–something to eat?"

"No, thank you. With the guidance of the Holy Spirit, I'd like to prompt you through deliverance techniques you learned at Rapha and I learned through Making Peace with Your Past."

"Okay."

"Are you ready?"

"Um...I guess so."

"Father, we come before You to give You honor and praise. Thank You, Lord, for all the work You are doing in Faith and Daphne's life. We ask You for Your perfect will to be done in her life. We ask for complete and total healing. Holy Spirit, please guide us through the steps of healing. Please bring to mind all Daphne needs to acknowledge and give to You. We ask this in Jesus' name."

"Yes, Lord. Please give me the strength and courage to go through the fire of remembering the past and moving beyond it. Be with me, Jesus, as we go through this. Show us where to begin. What do I need to forgive first?" We silently wait for the Holy Spirit. We don't have to wait long.

"I see Mother standing in front of the church. 'Daphne, would you come up here and help Mother lead the congregation in a round?'"

"A ROUND! Doesn't she know how hard it is to sing a round and she wants me to help lead it?? I can't believe this is happening to me! This is even worse than getting up and singing!"

"You need to forgive your mother, Daphne."

"Do I have to? She was awful! She was always thinking of how we had to measure up to being a preacher's family–and we never could!

"Mother is displeased. 'You're filthy! Go wash up before someone sees you. Get me a comb so I can comb your hair again. Why can't you keep it combed? Just look at these rats.' Yank and pull. 'I have half a mind to just shave it off!

"'Sit up straight! Mind your manners! Say hi to the grannies. Go play with the children and play nice.' Nag, nag, nag. All for the sake of appearance. 'No, no, no. You can't do that! You can't wear that! You can't be that! You're a preacher's kid!'" Oh, the pain of remembering. Tears. Endless tears.

"You need to forgive your mother, Daphne."

"Forgive her? For making me feel exposed and frightened? For all the anxiety and fear of failure?"

"All of it."

"Why?"

"Unforgiveness keeps you bound to abuse and your abuser. It's as though you're sitting in a boat trying to sail away from the past. Sailing away, not running. Sailing to freedom from all the pain of abuse. From bitterness, anger, resentment, vengeance, and any other emotion that accompanies them. They're on the dock your boat is tied to.

"You can try to run away by starting the engine and going as fast as you can, but you won't go anywhere. You must turn and face the issues on the dock. You'll only be able to cut the rope through forgiveness and giving up what you think is your right to vengeance. Once you're no longer in bondage, you'll find the healing you're seeking."

"I don't want to forgive her. What she did was wrong and I have a right to be angry."

"Yes, what she did was wrong and you did have the right to be hurt and angry. Anyone would be. It makes me very sad and angry that you weren't loved and treated the way you should have been.

"But vengeance belongs to God. Not you. Anger doesn't hurt your perpetrators. It only hurts you and keeps you chained to their abuse for as long as you hang on to it."

"But I don't feel like forgiving her."

"You don't have to feel like forgiving. Forgiveness is not a feeling. It's a command. You choose to do it as an act of obedience to God. The decision to forgive is like a train engine. Feelings are the caboose. Forgiveness leads and feelings follow."

"All right...I choose to forgive you, Mother, for...

"Father, I'm so ashamed for worrying about unreturned calls. For falling into the trap of trying to please man so soon after You showed me Your love. I can't believe I could ever need anyone's acceptance after all You give me. Forgive me for falling so soon."

"Daphne, you need to forgive yourself," Vivien encourages.

"I forgive you, Daphne, for being weak. I forgive you for seeking man's approval."

"Give the sin to Jesus. Give Him the shame."

"Jesus, I give You the debt of wanting to please man. I give You the shame of the debt of that sin. Take this shame from me, I give it completely to You...

"I'm holding my daddy's hand going to church. I am skipping and singing, happy to be with Daddy, even as he visits with someone else.

"'Faith, how would you like to sing a song for Daddy tonight?'

I shrug. "Okay? It never entered my mind before to perform to please him.

"Standing in front of all those people—all those eyes watching me. I never noticed so many people before! I'm scared stiff! I want to run and hide. I feel like I'm standing there before all those staring faces with no clothes on!

"What if I fail? Daddy wouldn't like that! What if my voice cracks or I forget the words!? Words! What words? I don't even know what song to sing! My knees are shaking and I feel like I might fall. My dress is almost soaked with sweat!

"I can't sing well enough to be here! I'm not worthy to be up here in front of everyone! But Daddy wants me to sing. It will please him if I sing pretty. I'll try just for him. I'll sing my very best just for him so he'll be proud of me...

"Swew! I made it. I can't believe I made it! Hey, they liked it—shaky voice and all! I was good and they really liked it. Wow!"

"Daphne, tell your daddy how he made you feel," Vivien encourages.

"That was extremely embarrassing, Daddy. How could you do that to me? I was so happy just to be with you, why couldn't you be happy to be with me? You didn't even give me any warning or anything! I didn't even have time to prepare something! You didn't even ask me if it was something I would like to do! You made me mad and ashamed!" Crying, I grab a tissue and blow my nose.

"Now you need to forgive him for making you perform and for shaming you."

"I forgive you, Daddy, for making me perform."

"And for shaming you."

"I forgive you for shaming me."

"You need to forgive your dad's church members for lavishing you with too much praise and for their part in giving you a spirit of performance. For compelling you to become self-centered and enslaved to performance."

"I forgive you, Daddy, and all the congregation for giving me a spirit of performance. I rebuke performance in the name of Jesus. Leave me and never come back!"

"You need to forgive your peers."

"I forgive the debt of my peers' expectations. I forgive them for putting me above them. Father, I forgive my peers for feeding my princess attitude by allowing me to control them. I forgive myself for my attitude and for being controlling."

"Forgive yourself for using your peers and for enjoying it so much."

OUCH! "I forgive you, Daphne..."

"Forgive for all the other negative emotions your daddy put on you. Come against the spirit that continues to keep you in the bondage of those emotions."

"I forgive Daddy for...I come against..."

"Forgive yourself for accepting the sin and the bondage that accompanied them."

"I forgive myself..."

"Do you need to forgive God for allowing the situation to happen?"

"I don't know, do I? How can I forgive God?"

"Are you upset with God for allowing it?"

"Yes."

"God has done nothing to forgive. He doesn't need your forgiveness. However, your perception perceives He has caused or allowed your pain. You may respectfully acknowledge your anger to God. Choosing to forgive Him will enable you to let go of your anger toward Him."

"God, I'm really angry that You allowed my daddy to treat me so badly. I choose to forgive You for allowing Daddy to make me perform for him and Your sake. Forgive me for being angry with You and blaming You for my father's sin."

The process continues. It's finally time to address Daddy's sexual abuse.

"...I love you, Daddy. You're everything to me. Why would you touch me there–that way–and make me touch you? That's nasty! I don't want to do that!

"'It would please me. I love you. Let me make you feel good. See, it feels good. If you love me, you'd want to make me feel good, too.'" It hurts! The memory is unbearable! I grab another tissue and dry the tears streaming down my face. The empty wastebasket is now half full. Vivien suggests we ask Jesus where He is while this is happening to me.

"Jesus, I need You. Please show Yourself to me."

After a brief silence, Vivien speaks as the Holy Spirit prompts, "Come, My child. Let Me shelter you from this awful sin."

"Make him stop! Why don't You make him stop? How can You let this happen to me?"

"My Father allows people the choice to obey or not. This is one reason sin is so bad–because it hurts the sinner and others. It hurts Me, too. This is why I left My home in heaven. To deliver those who are slaves to sin and Satan's hold on their lives. My blood of mercy covers even this situation.

"I have protected you from these memories all these years. I've been preparing for this very moment when you could receive My grace to overcome this. This, and every offense committed against you. All sin is forgiven. You must also forgive."

"But why?"

"In acknowledgment and acceptance of My forgiveness. You must realize it is for everyone. You cannot accept forgiveness for yourself and not for all. You cannot be forgiven if you will not forgive."

"Wouldn't forgiving be saying what he did was acceptable or okay? He deserves to be punished for what he did to me!"

"Punishment is not yours to give. It is Mine. Nursing pain and anger hurts no one but yourself–and Me."

"I can't do it on my own. I just can't forgive him for that."

"No, but I can and have. You can accept it."

"Does this mean he got to go to heaven after doing such a thing?"

"ALL sin is forgiven. It's a matter of repentance and accepting My forgiveness. However, that's between your father and Me. We're dealing with your sins now."

"My sins!?"

"Yes, your sins. Unresolved anger, malice, unforgiveness, seeking vengeance, bitterness. Need I continue, or can you think of a few on your own?"

"You're right." I'm wailing now. "Oh Father, please forgive me for my sins...as I choose to forgive my father."

"I have forgiven you. Now forgive yourself as well."

"Oh Lord, I'm so appalled to see what a terrible person I've been. Forgiving myself right now is even harder! I forgive you, Daphne."

"I spent my whole life judging others; I never realized how great my sins are. I'm so unworthy of Your love and forgiveness. Please wash away my sin and filth. I need You as my Lord and Savior. Please come into my heart and be my Lord and Savior."

"I was waiting for you to ask. It is done."

I quietly rest in His mercy and grace for several minutes. "Vivien, do you suppose she's sincere or just acting to look good?"

"You'd know, Faith."

"I'll check and see...Wow! I believe she's truly sincere! Cool!"

Time will tell.

Journal Entry – early pm

Viv came for a prayer session–wasted no time in delving into the debris. Often during the session, I felt like we were rushing things, but in truth, I think it was just my way of putting on the brakes. It amazes me that I did not feel emotionally exhausted afterward. Generally, I would have fallen straight into bed after a similar two-hour therapy session. I feel light as a feather–as though discarding heavy baggage. Wow! What a difference! It's just so much easier when we give it to the Holy Spirit in prayer sessions!

Began with Daphne. The magnitude of her unquenchable need for the entire world to love her was overwhelming. Giving it to Jesus–who is the only One who could love her enough anyway–was a major step for her.

What I find amazing is that the Holy Spirit revealed *all* sin during the session. While forgiving each offender He also exposed my sin that needed confessing and repenting. Wow!

Forgiving myself (Daphne) was one issue with a lot of pain. I just didn't think I could do it!

In the name of Jesus–I forgive you, Daphne, for controlling others and enjoying the process.

I was surprised God didn't have us start with sexual abuse. He had so many other debts He wanted Daphne to forgive way before she even thought about the sexual abuse.

- Forgiving Mother: jealousy, hate, emotional abuse.
- Forgiving Daddy: perform (sing, play piano, teach Sunday School)
- Forgiving myself for enjoying and responding to sexual contact released the notion that I could have in some way seduced Daddy. It cleansed me of feeling like I was the one committing the wrong.

By the time we had come to these issues, the process had become a well-oiled machine led by His Majesty, King Jesus.

I expected the pain level to be intolerably high. It's surprisingly not. Maybe in part because of so much previous work. Or because forgiving had become so much easier with each offense forgiven. Probably both.

Oh, what an awesome God!

Journal Entry – later pm

Daphne is recovering from last night's surgery. She's having many bandages removed. Jesus is choosing which to remove. He kisses every hurt. The healing injuries shine with new skin.

She loves looking at Him, being in His presence. He is so good, so beautiful. And He loves her! He truly loves her! She shakes her head once again in wonder that He has not forgotten her, not abandoned her. Holding His hand with love so deeply charged between the two leaves no need for conversation.

Love, pure love. But on Daphne's part a slowly maturing love as He shows the true nature of His character. Especially as she realizes how very much He has forgiven.

He has been revealing to her that He alone can say to her, "Yes, I understand how you feel." No one on earth can honestly say that! How very precious this is to us! Each time she sees this truth it overwhelms her again. She's realizing He actually suffered *with* her. He's giving her gifts to deal with the offense at the time of occurrence and even experiencing it on the cross.

Thank You, Jesus!

Journal Entry

Lord, thank You for the prayer session we had last night. Please bring to mind anything I have not recorded yet that You want me to write down. I remember the process continued even after Vivien and I hung up the phone. You kept working.

There was one instance where I can't remember the debt, but dealing with it was automatic. I remember realizing it as it happened. You brought up a debt, I cast out spirits in Your name and forgave the debt, debtor, and myself. All in a split second! Wow! It took longer to write it down than to take care of it! Is that how it's supposed to work all the time? When pain is present, invite the Holy Spirit to expose debts.

- Debts I have or have not forgotten are exposed.
- Cast out demons associated with offense so the bond between me and the offense is broken.
- Forgive sin. Sin is a transgression of God's law and deserves the death penalty. Jesus Christ paid for all sins on the cross. My forgiveness says perpetrators don't owe me for their sins. I forfeit my "right" for vengeance, leaving it in God's hands.
- Forgive the debtor, releasing the anger like cutting the rope to an anchor, so I can move on.
- Forgive self-releasing guilt.
- Repent for bitterness, harbored anger, etc.
- Ask where Jesus was in the situation so I can see His grace and mercy in action.

The process is not a magic formula. It's listening to the Holy Spirit and obeying.

My feelings jump all over the place, coming and going at will. Sometimes emotions are immediate and I weep uncontrollably-allowing feelings to flow.

When I didn't want to forgive I had to make a conscious effort to give it to Jesus. Vivien's word picture of the decision being a train engine followed by the caboose of emotion helped a lot. It also helped knowing forgiveness isn't a matter of making excuses for sin. It's giving the situation to God (and the governing authorities, if necessary) to take care of.

Forgiveness for others followed after the Holy Spirit convicted me of sins I needed to repent of. This shocked me at first. My victim mindset of self-pity insisted these terrible deeds were done to poor little ole me! It never occurred to *moi* that I could have sinned at any time during the situation! Of course, He's right and I can't deny or argue, so I comply.

Wow! How complete are Your works, O God Almighty! Just and pure are Your ways! Your truth does reach past my heart–into the deepest part of me and speaks the truth so clearly. Arguing with the Sword of Truth would be ludicrous.

Lord, please direct my steps. Should I go to group, spend more time in prayer, or time with Josh? Should I sleep? Which errands should I run? Which can wait? Please direct my steps. Please let me obey You today, Father.

Music.

Okay. To the piano–time for worship. Loving You time, how could I forget?

The words "How wonderful You are"–the expression! What a melody. Trying to express how speechless Your love makes me. So unworthy of You, Lord–yet so completely loved.

Feel prompted to spend some time writing songs today. Whew! Lord–that one seems hard with all the errands on my mind, as well as other decisions. Writing will be difficult but You're the One who brought it up, Lord. Please give me the oomph and tenacity to just do it!

I come against the spirit of laziness and the fear of failure in the name of Jesus. I come against the spirit of defeat over unmet potential. WHOA! That's a big one! In the name of Jesus–go away spirits of failure and defeat. I come against confusion that would consider writing as a low priority in the name of Jesus.

Satan, in the name of Jesus Christ of Nazareth, you must take your grip off–Yes OFF!–my gifts in the name of Jesus. Get your talons out of my shoulders. You've been there so long. Got kind of comfortable, didn't you? HA! BE GONE in the name of Jesus. You may NOT return.

Jesus, please replace that spirit or yoke–or whatever it is–with a renewed vision of what You want me to write.

I come against doubt in the name of Jesus.

Wow, Lord. You're kickin' these spirits all around! Hallelujah!

Hi, Maymee.

Steve Doesn't Get It

Anger

Anger, I've embraced you in the past
Drawing you close to endure what I could not see.
The path of pain is too familiar to surrender.
Then He showed me He had been there
Sharing in the torment I called "life."
I screamed, "Why didn't You stop it?
Keep it from happening?
How dare You say You were there!"

An image appears in an instant,
I see Him during the horrid abuse,
Tears streaming down His face–Sharing it all with me!
Oh, how He must have loved me to do that!
And I saw at that same moment
He had given me gifts to help me cope.

Knowing He was with me caught me by surprise.
No one could feel my solitude like He.
I thought of the cross where He bore my sin
And the sins of my abusers.
He had already forgiven them when He forgave me.
Are some sins worse than others?

So take His hand, Anger,
and the three of us will walk together
the path to restoration and healing.
And He, God Almighty, will make us strong!

> Turn to me and be gracious to me,
> for I am lonely and afflicted.
> The troubles of my heart are enlarged;
> Bring me out of my distresses.
> Look at my misery and my trouble,
> And forgive all my sins.
> Look at my enemies, for they are many,
> And they hate me with violent hatred.
> Guard my soul and save me;
> Do not let me be shamed,
> for I take refuge in You.
> Let integrity and uprightness protect me,
> For I wait for You.
>
> Psalm 25:16-21 (NASB)

1997

Journal Entry – a.m.

Feeling very grouchy, wanting to cry. Think I'm probably switching because I feel disoriented and confused.

Today was a church day. A little anxious about taking all of us to church. But in light of all Jesus has been doing, felt confident in Him, so took a chance. Guess I knew if Daphne needed protection He would provide it for her.

Worship service was so awesome. We surely entered in and loved His Majesty, King Jesus! Whew! Wow!

Annie wants some candy. Not sure what's happening here. Maybe she also needs to come out and play or have somebody talk to her as Annie.

"Hi, Viv. It's me, Daphne. I don't know why I'm feeling down after being with Jesus and everything. It seems like I should be completely healed by now!"

"Perhaps you have a void that needs to be filled with wholesome father images."

"I'm afraid to ask. It may bring more emotional pain."

"I'm hoping you'll receive joy and laughter instead."

"I guess I'm trying to control the situation."

"Shall we pray?"

"Okay."

"Father in heaven, I'm so excited for all the work You're doing in Daphne. I'm excited about the healing that's been taking place in her. Jesus, please show Daphne Your Father and re-parent her like You did Baby Daphne. Fill her so full of Your love there will be no lacking in her life. Give her an overflow of joy and laughter as You show her how You wish she had been parented. Better yet, how You, Yourself would have raised her."

"Jesus, thank You for revealing to me now that I control out of fear! I come against fear in the name of Jesus Christ of Nazareth!

"Viv, Annie wants to talk to you for a little bit."

"Okay."

"Hi, Vivie."

"Hi, Annie. How are you doing?"

"Fine."

"Are you still at the banquet with Jesus?"

"No, silly, because I'm out here!"

Journal Entry – p.m.

Viv prayed with Daphne today, asking Jesus to reparent her the way He would have.

Annie wanted to talk to Vivie too, but Annie feels like Vivie wants Annie to go play–or go eat–and not bother anybody. Annie feels like nobody likes her.

We are so very, very tired. No nap today–time with Josh, instead.

Jesus, Your strength is what I need to work with Daphne and Annie. I love being here with You during this wonderful time of quiet. Thank You for providing this time. The weekend had so many distractions–taking my time from You.

Let me face this reparenting issue, Father, if that's what You want. You know what is best. I will wait on You...

Jesus enters the room.

My Lord! My heart quickens as He draws me near, kissing my hand. His hugs are so safe.

Daphne, want to go to the park with Annie and Me?

Do you want that of me, my Lord?

No, the question is, do you want that of Me? Do you want Me to redo the father-daughter past that you did not have–fill you with new memories of your childhood?

I–I don't know. You have always known what's best for me. How can I begin to ask You for such a thing–or even begin to know if I need it?

Oh, Daphne, how you've grown!

Really?

Yes! Trusting Me without trying to be the One in control! That's good!

Thank You. You are the One who is teaching me, remember? Free lessons.

Yes! Free lessons! I love You, Daphne!

I love You, my Lord! I want to spend time with You–let You continue to love me. Is that all right?

Yes, I love our time together, too.

His overwhelming love–secure love–never changing–is always there. I'm constantly amazed at His steadfast love. I hope He will hold me for the next million years. Maybe He will!

Even when Annie wasn't the one working in the front–out here–our sense of taste has been greatly enhanced. We continue to eat smaller, more regular meals. I listen to Annie and the body when she is hungry–apologizing when we get too hungry. It's been surprising to me that for some reason food tastes a lot better and I'm able to fully enjoy it.

We checked in on Annie briefly during the past couple of days. Found with delight that she was curled up in the Father's lap. A contented look on her chocolate and spaghetti sauce daubed face. Funny, Jesus wearing white robes, and He is not concerned at all with her messy state.

Then for some reason, Annie wanted out tonight and needed to be acknowledged. Viv asked her why she wasn't still at His banquet table. She said she didn't know, but she obviously knew she could not be there and be out at the front.

Let's ask Jesus why Annie is out front.

There are no locks on the doors of the House of Love. I let her come and go as she wants.

Please reveal, Lord Jesus, what we need to do for Annie.

She needs to play. Let her come out and play with all her toys. Let her be the little girl she is, for now, anyway.

But what about therapy, Lord?

This IS therapy. With Annie, you are going to learn patience.

Hmmm, okay.

Annie is going to heal in a very different way than Daphne.

Oh?

She is a different personality with a completely different story. Trust Me on this, Faith.

Okay, Jesus. You truly are the One in control. It feels like Viv and I want to rush things a bit.

Yes, and this is going to take a little bit of getting to know Annie. You knew Daphne so much better because she was such a predominant personality. With Annie, you've only begun to get to know her and find out her needs.

Teach me, Lord. I am willing.

Let Annie out to play. Observe her as you would a three-year-old in play therapy. Much will be learned by how she plays.

Wow! Okay.

Journal Entry – a.m.

When Annie was faced with writing in the journal she drew a large face with solid colored blocks for eyes and a large oval mouth.

Annie is really in a lot of pain right now. It's her turn to receive therapy and time with Jesus. Last night it felt as though Annie was gonna burst if she couldn't come out and play.

Steve returned home from church about the time I finished writing. I asked if he would talk to Annie and play with her. He said he wanted to talk to Faith first. Annie felt he didn't believe she even existed and he obviously did not want to play with or acknowledge her. She began to become anxious.

Steve said he wanted me to organize a plan for our bills. I said I felt it was much too stressful for me to handle and asked him to stand in the gap. He began to cycle into hopelessness and anger. I, in turn, became very frustrated with him. I told him he was a big boy, he could handle it.

He went into the bedroom and proceeded to throw things around in the guise of getting the bills together. He began shouting and cursing at himself and the entire situation.

Annie and the other children inside me were terrified of being abused. We called Vivien and prayed with her. I knew Annie could not come out then. She wouldn't be safe with him so angry. I showed her a couple of children's books. I got the baby doll and took us all to bed to protect us from the Danger Man. Annie was so very disappointed she did not get to play. But she didn't want to be out because she was so afraid.

Today, I felt closed in and withdrawn from Steve because of last night. We weren't sure if he was still angry.
– Faith

"Dr. Kathy speaking."

"Hello, Dr. Kathy. This is Faith. I really need to talk. I'm having problems with Steve and Annie."

After I've explained what happened, Dr. Kathy asks, "May I speak to Annie?"

"I really don't want to talk right now. I don't want to come out. I will NEVER come out with that man around EVER AGAIN! He scares me. I'm afraid he'll hurt me."

"Steve probably only acted that way because he was under a lot of stress. Do you understand?"

"NO. All I wanted was for him to talk to me and give me hugs and let me know he believes I'm here. It hurts that he doesn't believe in me."

"The other inside people need to come and hug you and play with you. They can help a lot."

"I want REAL hugs. In-the-flesh kind of hugs and somebody out there to believe in me and let me tell my story. I'M REALLY MAD at Steve for not trying to get to know me. Vivie and Dan try more than HIM!"

Journal Entry – p.m.

Called Dr. Kathy and had a telephone session. She talked to Annie briefly, but Annie was reluctant to come out for long because she was afraid of Steve. Annie and I, Faith, both were very angry at Steve for not making any effort to understand what was going on with us.

As soon as we finished talking to Dr. Kathy, Melissa came out and took over. She cuddled with Steve on the couch and initiated sex with him. At first, he was confused and reluctant, but she convinced him she wasn't the one angry with him. She genuinely wanted to make love to him then. They had a great time.

Then Steve said...

"So who was that who just climaxed, Annie?"

GASP! Intense fury fills us so much I'm afraid if we slap him—as we'd like to—with the force of all our joined anger we'd kill him!

"NEVER speak of the children in reference to our sex life—EVER—EVER AGAIN! The children are not capable of sexual activity! Where have you BEEN all this time?!"

Steve went to the hospital to visit his dad. Silence is so nice while dressing. Must plan ways for Annie to play. Maybe we'll watch "Beauty and the Beast."

Tears swell. It's okay to come out, Annie. Come out and cry.

Vivie has difficulty relating to Annie so she tried to call someone else, but they weren't home. Annie felt so alone. She finally found someone to talk to. After a few minutes, she calmed down and stopped crying.

"Dr. Kathy speaking."

"Hello, Doctor. This is Faith. Steve and I just had another big fight. He's just been humoring us all along in sessions. He doesn't believe any of us exist. He does not want to understand it. It's difficult, so he won't even look at it.

"Faith is so tired of doing all his thinking for him. Now that she has so much going on in the system she's making therapy and healing with God a priority."

"Steve is having to do more for himself–like business calls, figuring bills, et cetera." Excuses, excuses.

"He wants her back the way she was when she was doing all that stuff for him. That was easier for him. I MARRIED A DUMB JERK! WHY? WHY WAS I ATTRACTED TO SOMEONE WHO CAN'T EVEN THINK?"

"There had to be a reason."

"The only thing I can come up with is he seemed safe to me. He was nothing like my daddy. That's what I was looking for, the opposite of Daddy."

"Maybe Melissa should lovingly explain to him about the multiplicity."

"Well, it would have to be her because nobody else in here even likes him. After he and Faith fought several of us were extremely angry with him. Melissa seduced him last night and had wonderful sex with him. It made no sense to us, but was perfectly logical to her."

"That's normal for Melissa. She was created to love him without the hang-ups about the sexual abuse."

"But then he said what he did about Annie! We were livid! We almost slapped him. I think he could tell by the look on our face he had seriously messed up. Of course, Faith let him have it good!"

Journal entry – a.m.

Feels like a new personality may be emerging–time will tell. Been depressed in comparison to yesterday with all this new Annie stuff.

Jesus, I feel crazy. Please give me a mind like Yours. Lord, I give Annie to You. Please direct the steps You want taken to help her heal. Please hold Annie, Jesus. Would You please send someone with skin on to hug and love her, too? I'm glad You understand.
– Faith

Journal Entry – mid-day

Rough couple of days around here. Can't think very clearly today. Trying to read the Word but very hard to concentrate.

Annie got to watch two Disney movies yesterday. She had a hard time last night. Steve was visiting his dad at the hospital, but he would have made it worse, anyway. He doesn't understand Annie or her needs.

He's in there now "trying to read" volume one of our diary. I hear him flipping the pages quickly, just to be going through the motions. He's overwhelmed at how many pages there are to read. I told him to only read one or two at a time. Obviously, he didn't listen. He does that all the time. I'll say something, then he'll pretend to understand and then act like he didn't get the message. Maybe he just doesn't care.

He only gets the significance of the matter when I rant and rave. Then I'm distressed because I let myself get angry. And he's upset and intimidated by my anger. However, he does remember the issue longer.

Today I need to be alone and quiet. Steve is here–no work today. Father, only by Your grace. I need to be more supportive of Steve–with his dad dying and the stress of finding a job. I just want to scream at him to go away and leave me alone. In my strength, Lord, I'm pretty washed up. Only by Your grace can I have any compassion for my husband. Help me, Jesus.

I'm wondering if Daphne has integrated now or if Jesus is still working with her. Annie is the one screaming for love and attention.

Jesus, please love Annie today. Please hold her close. I need Your Holy Spirit to shine on Annie today.

Maymee is not very prominent. Must nurture her with music. Mass choir rehearsal is tomorrow night. I think she'll be excited.

"Turn that blasted honky tonk music off!" Steve grouses. "That noise gets on my nerves!"

"If I knew you were such a bigot I'd never have married you!"

"If you're supposed to be black you'd have been born with dark skin."

"You're a red-neck!"

"You're just flaunting the being black part to get back at your dad."

"That makes no sense! My daddy's dead."

"Maymee has an attitude."

"You're the one with an attitude! Now the truth comes out about how you really feel. I don't think you believe any of us exist!"

"When will I get Faith back? Eight-ten more years?"

"You certainly aren't helping matters with the way you're acting! I want to slap your face all the way to Ohio!"

"If you can't deal with what I'm going through we can always get a divorce. Of all people, I need you to try to understand what's going on!"

"Do you think I enjoy going through all this–that I'm making it up for attention or something?"

He shrugs his shoulders. OOOH! HE DOES THAT A LOT! I'm *cursing* mad now!

"No WAY would I make ANYTHING up! Did I choose to be Maymee? No, but she's there and she's black. Why can't you accept her?"

"I didn't marry a black person."

"You're such a bigot! Well part of me is black so you're just going to have to deal with it!"

He doesn't even know about Joey and Nathan. The content of what he doesn't know would fill the cosmos!

Journal Entry – p.m.

After our fight about personalities, Steve came home and told me he was on my side. We endured him through bedtime and tried to stay warm in our cold bedroom. He probably wanted some extra kisses, but he hadn't shaved in about 24 hours. Yuk! So I told him good night but helped keep his stupid feet warm.

Journal Entry

Crying a lot this morning–trying to hang in there alone. Getting breakfast for Annie and music for Maymee. Felt Annie and Maymee both very strongly. Probably switching a lot.

Very upset every time I think about the Franklin choir thing. Maymee senses how needy Annie is. She believes

Annie's emotional state will keep Maymee from attending the rehearsals. We want someone else to go with us. Some support in the flesh, but can't think of anyone to ask. I want to call the church to ask if anyone from the choir has expressed interest, but need my emotions in check first. Feeling too much shame for being emotionally needy.

And so, Jesus, I come to You this morning–so desperately in need of You. I'm so lacking in any emotional stability. Thank You for being my Rock.

I know in coming to You I'm supposed to praise You first, so please forgive me, Lord. I'm rushing in right now to cry HELP at the top of my lungs. Lord, You are the only One who can deliver me out of my insanity.

Steve can't be there for me. Dr. Kathy is there, but she doesn't have Your healing power. Vivien's willing to pray, but she can only comprehend so much, especially with the young ones. Dan's buried in music. But Lord, even if all these people had the answers and the power to help–they have no power to heal as You do. Please forgive me when I lean on them before leaning on You. You alone are Almighty God–who can and is healing me! You're the One!

Just for today, this very hour, Jesus, please give me strength. I give it to You in small increments of time because that's where I'm at today. Thank You for being here holding my hand–holding me, period! I need You, Jesus!

Will I ever be able to sing for You at church again, Lord? Maymee would really like to sing "I Need Thee Every Hour." We all think about "Via Dolorosa." Will Dan let her sing or will he think she's too emotionally unstable?

Direction from You, Lord. What do You want me to do with Annie or Maymee–or this new one coming up?

Prepare a welcome for the new personality.

Okay, Lord! Wow!

Give her a tour of the system like you would a guest in your home. Let her know you are all conscious and trying to achieve a common goal. Let her know she is safe. Create a safe place for her inside if she needs it. Introduce her to Me and leave a ministering angel with her always. Dispel all curses and evil spirits attached to her in My name.

Thank You, Father.

Let Annie play and Maymee sing today. If they need to cry it's all right. I'm here.

Yes, You are here! My, what a God!

Spiritual Nourishment

My Jesus Knew What I Needed

My Jesus knew what I needed to know
before I knew it.
He knew the next step I'd take before I took it.
If I listen to His still small voice
I know He'll help me make the right choice.

My Jesus knows what I need to know,
before I do it.
His grace is enough for every need I have.
His love is greater than any love I've ever had.
His wisdom is much greater than any we have.
That's why I know He knows
what I need to know before I do it.

His grace, His love, His wisdom are all I need to hear
How He provides everything.
I know He knows what I need to know
before I know it!
He knows every thought I make
and every step I take.
He knows what I need to know before I do it!

He waters the mountains from His upper chambers;
The earth is satisfied with the fruit of His works.
He causes the grass to grow for the cattle,
And vegetation for the labor of mankind,
So that they may produce food from the earth,
And wine, which makes a human heart cheerful,
So that makes his face gleam with oil,
And food, which sustains a human heart.

Psalm 104:13-15 (NASB)

1997

"Hello?"

"Hello. Is this Paul?"

"Yes, it is."

"This is Viv's friend, Faith. Thank you for letting me call. I know you've been mentoring Viv in prayer sessions with me and I wanted to talk to you myself."

"Okay."

"Do you think you could help me make my husband understand about the multiplicity?"

Paul chuckles. "Every generation of women is optimistic. They think men will change, but in truth, men are ogres.

We've always been ogres and we probably always will be ogres."

Ha! Ha! Ha!

"You need to release him from understanding any of it. Let him be your husband, not your pastor, friend, or counselor. He can't be anyone but your husband."

"Okay. Annie wants to talk with you. Is that okay?"

"Sure."

"Hi, Paul."

"Hi, Annie. How are you?"

"Sad and lonely. Nobody likes me."

"Jesus loves you. Do you know Jesus?"

"Yes. He's nice. He had a party just for me and let me eat anything I wanted at His banquet table. I have to check out what He says He can be to me. He says He can always love me and never leave or forsake me. What does forsake mean?"

"It means you can trust Him and He will never betray your trust."

"NO ONE AT ALL can be trusted!"

"Jesus is different. He's the *only* One who *can* be completely trusted. Would you like Jesus to be your friend?"

"Okay."

"You have to ask Him."

"What do I say?" Whispering.

"Jesus…"

"Jesus..."

"Will You..."

"Will You..."

"...be my friend?"

"...be my friend?"

"What did He say?"

"He said 'YES!'"

"What is He doing?"

"Sitting on the floor. He wants me to come and play."

"He does?"

"Yes! He said He wants to be my friend and He wants us to play!" Giggle. "I'm gonna play with Jesus now–okay? Bye!" Click. Giggling, laughing, squealing coming from the playroom. Annie and Jesus, hugging a teddy bear, wrestle on the floor.

We have an eye doctor's appointment, Annie. We need to take a bath now.

Ah, Mama! Do we have to? I'm having fun with Jesus!

I'll let you play in the tub...

Oh Boy!

Annie sings loudly all around the house, finding each article of clothing needed. The pets are excited because they notice a child is at large. They anticipate getting played with.

Joey drives to the doctor's office so Annie can sing in the truck. She gets a couple of odd glances but doesn't care.

She's getting to play in the company of what appears to be a "safe" friend.

We get glasses. Cheap ones. Ugly! Maybe someday we will get some pretty ones. I don't mind as long as I can see.

I want a taco–so Taco Bell it is.

OW! Too hot! It's too spicy.

I'm sorry. Next time I'll get you a hamburger.

Yum! I like hamburgers!

Afraid to go to choir tonight. Don't want to cry the entire time. Jesus, please let Steve get home so he can go with me.

Journal Entry

Thank you. Late to choir, but Steve stayed with me.

Annie went to choir tonight in a ponytail, with no makeup, and ugly glasses, but it didn't bother her any. She panicked when she couldn't find Steve after church. Steve had Faith's letter to Dan telling him all God is doing. She couldn't find Steve anywhere so she sat by the door and cried a little because she was alone and afraid. Faith was nervous that someone would come and talk to her and notice she was Annie. That didn't happen. We are all so glad!

Faith gave Dan a copy of Daphne's story, the miracle part. Hope he can decipher the handwriting and follow the conversations. Please, Lord, give him a vision of what miracles You're working in me!

Tomorrow night is the rehearsal for the Martin Luther King mass choir! I wonder what God will work in us tomorrow. Each day I am tempted not to work or document as much and sometimes "fudge," skimming on details. It's work that's for sure! Lord, please help me stick to it!

Journal Entry

Maymee is absolutely satisfied tonight! The MLK choir rehearsal was really good for her. It was non-stop singing–clapping–praising Jesus. She is so content that she is silent–at peace with her God and her world.

Somehow the experience did not drain the body and emotions like Faith thought it would. I wonder if it's because Maymee doesn't have Daphne's performance baggage. She just loves to sing about Jesus.

We didn't have a quiet day alone with Jesus today, but our steps were ordered by Him. I sense His peace tonight more than I have in quite a while.

Thank You, Lord, for your peace. I love You, Jesus. The weekend is here again, Lord. How I need Your strength. Didn't want to take Steve to work and keep the truck, but have to pick up Josh this afternoon. Help me remember, Jesus.

Steve watched the last part of "The Little Princess" with me last night. Then somehow–even though we were on totally different pages–we started praying together. We poured out all our frustrations and emotions to the Lord.

We began to do battle in the spiritual realm. Flailing weakly at first with weapons that seemed too large. But then growing in His might to flat-out shove it all right back in the devil's face! We received a tiny glimmer of a vision of the ministry God has for us as we began to intercede for others. My heart went "ding" as Steve named someone in need of our love and support. YES! It occurs to me it was Steve who led in prayer.

Wow! Thanks, Lord!

Both ended up thanking God for the mess–no car, no car payment, no car insurance, bills. We thanked God for the pain, the financial strain, issues with Josh, Steve's dad–everything. It was quite a prayer meeting.

Afterward, we talked about how we need to be united in battle each day. To rise up, put on our armor, and enter the battle together. Jesus is the only hope we have. We need Him for each laborious step.

Cried a lot, but the cleansing kind of tears. Giving my emotions to Jesus. I realize emotional stability is not there. I cry every day–sometimes over the smallest things. Tonight I gave that to Him too and asked Him for comfort when I feel crazy. Maybe He's teaching me to rely more on Him than on my feelings. With all my feelings, that's gonna take some doing!

New issues–probably more sexual abuse coming to memory. Either to Annie or to this new personality coming up. Resisting going to bed tonight. Tired, but not wanting to face the dark. So afraid.

Lord Jesus, please hold me as I sleep tonight. Let my dreams be only of You. Let any new pain coming up be only as Your hand allows. I give You the new information my subconscious is offering, knowing You will heal this wound, too. Use it to put me back together, not merely patched up–but totally new!

In the name of Jesus, I come against self-pity and fear.

Journal Entry

No dream work that I know of. I remember waking and saying something about the Holy Spirit. Probably much warfare going on last night.

Today I am very tired. Tempted to skip group and go back to sleep–for no other reason than pure exhaustion.

I think Daphne has integrated! So far her issues have not been there since we had the prayer session. Wouldn't that be awesome?

Lord, I give You me today. My emotions are so close to the surface. I feel like crying–from what? From lack of sleep, good and bad stress. Jesus, I need a black dress for Monday night's concert. Thank You, You will supply.

I give You the hair, Lord. HA! Only You can do somethin' to the hair!

Wow! What an arrangement. Oh, Jesus, the music doesn't get any better than this. Singing at Bethesda with Dan and now singing for MLK, Jr. Day in the best seats in the house! God, You're too good!

I love Maymee, Lord. Please let me keep a lot of her spirit when she integrates into me. Lord, I know You want me to be one whole person, but I'd almost rather be split than give up Maymee.

Good morning, Annie.

Umm. I'm sleepy, Mama.

I know it's kind of early. Wanna go to the banquet room for breakfast?

Yes, yes, yes! Hands clapping–waking up.

Okay. Wash up and we'll go.

Yum, yum, Mama. I want lots and lots.

Yes, what do you want to eat?

Father, please guide this session. Thank You, Lord.

It's time to teach you about the food on the table, Annie. You see, My food is food for the spirit as well as the body.
Milk–Like newborn babies, crave pure spiritual milk, so that by it you may grow in your salvation, now that you have tasted that the Lord
is good.
Fruit–...the fruit of the Spirit is love, joy, peace, patience, kindness, goodness, faithfulness, gentleness, and self-control.
Cheese–the growing process
Vegetables–to grow strong in His power
Hamburgers–Delight yourself in the Lord and He will give you the desires of your heart.
Bread–I am the Bread of Life.
Water–...whoever drinks the water I give him will never thirst. Indeed, the water I give him will become in him a spring of water welling
up to eternal life.

Thank You, Lord. I love You, Jesus.

Daphne's Integration

Water Flowing

Sunset on the river-such poetry-oh ecstasy.
If only I could send my spirit atop the water
Drenched in the sunset like a beautiful gown
Blending with the myriad of colors floating on endlessly.
Now a touch of orange-see the crimson?
Oh, how the Creator mixes His palette with expertise.

We draw it on paper. Paint it on boards.
Yet there is nothing to compare with each masterpiece
in the evening and each greeting at dawn.
I never lose the wonder of each sunset I see.

Look! Ah! And look again,
changing continuously-ever so slightly.
But when I look away I am astounded
at how great is the change.
If I were but one such masterpiece,
my life would be complete.

Blessed be to the LORD,
Because He has heard the sound of my pleading.
The LORD is my strength and my shield;
My heart trusts in Him, and I am helped;
Therefore, my heart triumphs,
And with my song I shall thank Him.

Psalm 28:6,7 (NASB)

1997

Journal Entry

Steve's Dad died late last night. This day has been the most stressful ever! My emotions have been extremely haywire. Feeling very disoriented and confused, depressed, anxious, nervous, angry—too much goin' on. No time to be alone and write or talk to the Lord today.

Skipped church since we were up so late last night and we thought we might need to go visit Steve's mom.

On overload all day, like I was going to self-destruct at any time. I feel so abandoned. Steve and Josh went fishing and didn't return when they said they would—made me nervous. Worked hard to fix lunch for us. Felt a great need for hugs.

Called Viv. She went to spend the weekend with a friend whose mother died. Won't return 'til Monday.

Called Linda–she's sick with the flu.

Called Phyllis–asked her if she could come over after church and just hug me. She said probably not because of the children. She hoped I understood. I didn't reply. I'm so angry with her. I thought she was my friend.

Called and asked Laura–or told her I needed hugs. She asked about the funeral and said she would give me my hug on Tuesday. Is anybody listening?

Shellie called–told her I needed a hug. She said she was sending one over the phone. Told her it was not good enough.

Tom brought a pretty plant over to take to the funeral, but I was on the phone. He didn't stay long enough for me to get a hug.

Complained loudly when Steve and Josh got home. Josh hugged me. Steve hugged me. I wanted more hugs.

Elenora was so sweet. She was helpful over the phone. I told her I was so confused and disoriented. I didn't know what to do about going to the funeral not knowing whether we were welcome or not. I want to support Steve's mom, but not be in the way or come if we're not wanted. So confusing.

My body is sore from last night's choir rehearsal. I ache all over. It was quite a workout. My back hurts.

I feel extremely crazy with very raw emotions. So fed up with people in general–their lack of caring or being available in person for us.

Why don't pastors make house calls anymore? Must we ask them specifically to come to our house to give us hugs and physical touch? Phones are nice, but whatever happened to up-close and personal? If Viv were in town I know she would be here.

It's disappointing and discouraging when others don't understand or know how to relate. They tend to distance themselves. Churchy cliches like "I know it's going to get better," "Have faith," or "I'm praying for you," are no replacement for empathy. Treatment groups are more supportive than my Christian friends. They can relate as we share similar experiences.

Don't even want to call Dr. Kathy. I feel since she's the doctor she's what Steve's friend calls a Rent a Friend.

Thank You, God, for Steve's friend who went with him to view the body. I couldn't go. Please forgive me, Lord, I am so angry and selfish right now. I need You with skin on, Jesus.

Not able at all to work on inside people today. Not sure who is at the front. Somebody who's pretty angry a lot of the time and doesn't like that we aren't getting what we want and feel we need. Probably Annie.

When people aren't there for me it brings up the pain of last year when I was to keep silent in group and how awful that felt. Nearly pushed me completely over the deep end!

When friends don't respond I wonder what I–or maybe one of my alters–has done to chase them away. Am I appearing to be insane? Makes me want to completely withdraw from them all so they won't have the chance to hurt me again.

Journal Entry

So very tired. The concert was great. Didn't get to see much of Kirk Franklin because his part didn't start until almost ten p.m. and I was exhausted. I'll get a tape.

Told Steve if I hadn't been so stressed out I would probably have stayed for the entire concert–no matter what. I came home at ten. Messed up hormones–emotions bonkers–Steve's dad dying–viewing body today–it's all too much. I feel bad today–my nerves are very much on edge. Steve said my tolerance level is almost zero. I told him I know, I'm sorry, but I couldn't help the way I was feeling. Gotta get help from the doctor for my hormones.

I hate being around anybody. My body hurts and noise bothers me. Riding in the truck is unbearable. Every bump we hit makes me cuss or grit my teeth. I've asked the Lord to forgive me for grumbling about the truck. It's what He has provided for us to use right now. Still, I hate riding in it. It grates on my nerves.

So very disappointed in friends. Tempted to write them all out of my life. Steve said a couple of them called. I didn't say anything, but thought screw them–I no longer have any friends. Viv and Elnora might be the only exceptions, but even they are capable of hurting me. So tired of loving people 'cause it hurts too much.

Journal Entry – a.m.

Steve's dad's funeral was this morning–stressful to get there on time. Steve's mom's family turned out to be very pleasant people. I liked her sisters.

Don't want to work on inside people today. I took our baby doll, teddy, rag doll, and a blankie for Annie and snoozed in the hammock in our backyard. It was warm. Got a slight chill around five, but she really liked that!

I felt like sitting in the rocking chair with the baby doll and rocking, but didn't. My mom used to sit in the pitch blackness, rocking, waiting for my daddy to come home. She was crazy. I am too, but in my unique way–not hers.

So depressed. Mad at God for all this happening.

Oh, God, how can we take any more? You show me such love. You teach us to pray–then WHAM! An elevated temperature in the furnace. Make it seven times hotter than before. Like the king commanded for Shadrach, Meshach, and Abednego. Well, I'm not sure I'm willing anymore. Sorry, I'm just *not* Your girl. You can *have* the whole mess. I GIVE UP!

Journal Entry – p.m.

At the river with Steve. He almost had to drag me out of the house, but I'm glad he did. Gave up fishing since all I've done is catch trees and lose hooks.

So what's going on with my inside people during all this funeral-related grown-up stuff going on? Of course, everyone's been in the back and not able to come out since almost a week ago. Faith is usually the presenting person when Josh comes home from the boys' home on weekends.

I did little things for some of my people during the week from hell. For Annie, I took along a teddy bear and a couple of toys, and a few pieces of hard candy to suck on. I wonder if I could sneak a couple of candy bars in for me without Annie knowing. Hmmm...does Annie ever sleep when she's not out front? For Maymee, I arranged our schedule so we could come back to town for the MLK concert.

My back has been hurting a lot. It seems to ease up when I take a nap. I kept forgetting I have pain meds.

More of You, Jesus! Less of me. Oh, how sick to my stomach am I with my problems and selfishness. Please forgive me, Father. You alone can make me whole again.

Lord, I believe as I stood looking out the kitchen window this morning You gave me reassurance about our house. I do believe. Help me overcome my unbelief! I love to hear Your voice. Let not doubt and fear distort Your message to my heart.

"Hi, Viv. I missed you so much! Steve's dad died Friday night."

"I'm sorry."

"I sure needed some hugs!"

"I wish I could have been here to give them to you. Do you want me to come give you one?"

"No, I'm okay now. I called several people to ask for a hug, but they wouldn't even consider it. They were too busy for just one little hug! I can't believe it! I thought they were my friends! HA! Some friends!"

"Are you going to forgive them?"

"Do I have to?"

"What do you think?"

"I have to. Okay, I forgive you, Phyllis and Laura, for not caring enough to take the time to comfort me when I was grieving. I forgive you for not being there for me when I needed you. Right now I feel like I'm under attack from the enemy and need to wage some warfare."

"Go for it!"

"I come against fear of rejection in the name of Jesus. I come against rebellion, incompetence, and addiction in the name of Jesus. Father, please protect me from these demons returning to taunt me. Amen.

"I don't understand why people-pleasing issues are resurfacing when Daphne seems to have integrated."

"Do you think it's possible other inside people might wrestle with the same issues?"

"It's possible. I just thought they were all Daphne's."

"You don't have to have DID to be concerned about what others think. Sometimes it just comes up in normal daily experiences."

"I see. Maybe it was just the level of pain associated with issues Daphne had about performance. For so many years in therapy, I've had things resurface after I thought they were dealt with. I guess I expect it to resolve itself naturally this time."

"When the Holy Spirit does the healing–it's a done deal. You have to choose to respond to it, though. God will only heal as much as you submit to. It depends on your focus. That's what 'taking every thought captive to the obedience of Christ means.'"

"You know, I believe the Holy Spirit is directing my therapy now. It's amazing to see the miracles He's been doing. I wonder how much of this is reaping the benefits of having worked for so long in therapy and how much of it is purely miraculous. But then, who can describe a miracle? Some miracles may take years to slowly make their way. Others are instantaneous reprieves."

"Well, you have released a lot of pent up anger toward perpetrators through therapy. You've replaced a lot of lies with truth, writing them in your mind. Now the Holy Spirit is making them real to you as He writes them on your heart."

"Hmmm!"

Journal Entry

Daphne's finale.

It is a fact that God took control of Daphne's prayer sessions. He gave her not what we thought she needed, but what He knew would work. It's so amazing how quickly and completely He performed this in Daphne.

So now, I look at the Daphne doll Steve and Josh gave me for Christmas on her stand on the piano. Instead of it invoking pain and tears, I see it as a symbol of the Daphne that used to be. I no longer hate or despise her, but now think of her memory with compassion.

WOW! She is truly integrated into me! I now have no inhibitions about writing songs and getting others' approval for them. The part of me that was Daphne was created to write. I now embrace that knowledge with satisfaction. Knowing I was created to write–that's all I need. Not man's approval because I'm not writing for man, but for God and myself.

As a natural outpouring of what is happening between my Creator and me. A State of the Union address of sorts. It frees me up in so many ways.

For example, bottom line, I am to write, period. Just write. That can include my diary, a book, poetry, essays, articles, or songs. I've struggled for years with the issue of writing songs. I've had such grand schemes in mind–such lofty ideals. Pooh!

God wants me to apply myself to become the best I can be as far as study and growth. My songs may never be any more than an expression of my life for God's purposes. One song may be to bless four or five different individuals, while another may touch only one. Still, others may be love songs between my God and me alone. The key is that I do what He has created in me to fulfill His purpose in me!

In my creative efforts, He has pleasant surprises in store. My responsibility is to catch as much of the creativity as possible when ideas come. No matter the inconvenience, even if inspiration comes in the middle of the night. My laziness has cost me some pretty good stuff. Forgive me, Lord.

Looking back, I realize only a week ago it felt like a new personality was emerging. That, or Annie was in a lot of pain and possibly getting ready to disclose some abuse she has not shared before now. The new personality could likely have been emotional upheaval from hormonal imbalance.

The stuff with Annie is real enough, though. Was afraid last week and am afraid now. Lord, please walk me through this new time–new pain–new healing. I am scared. Annie's scared, too.

Mama, it hurts.

I know, baby.

Nobody wanted to hug me. Didn't you say to ask for what I needed?

Yes, I did.

It didn't work. They didn't have their ears on yet. Like Mr. Potato Head, I couldn't find their ears.

You tried to put their ears on?

Yep! But some of them just didn't listen, Mama. Tears blur our vision.

That must have felt awful.

All I wanted was hugs–that's all–just hugs, Mama!

I know, Annie.

They brought food. Food, Mama! They said 'no' and 'hope you understand' when I asked for a hug. I DIDN'T UNDERSTAND! What's so hard about five minutes and a good hug?

You're angry.

Yes, Mama. I'm mad! I don't want to play with them or be their friend anymore. At all!

You don't want to be their friend?

NO! I NEEDED A HUG THEN! IT'S TOO LATE NOW!

Annie, sometimes people can't be there for us. Perhaps if they had a fax machine they could have faxed us a hug.

Hmm...I can pencil you in for a hug next Tuesday–or a month from this Thursday–at 6 p.m. No? Let's see–that won't work–how about 5:45 p.m.? Got a time frame for me? Two minutes, huh? Are you sure? You must be mistaken. That's all it takes for a hug? Well, in that case, I could probably give you one now!

HUMPH!

Jesus is the only One we can depend on.

MAYBE.

No, really, because He is the Son of God.

I know, Mama. You talk to Him all the time, but I wanted Him with skin on, ya know?

Sigh. Yes, I do. Sometimes people aren't listening to God or the people who need them.

Why?

I don't know. They just mess up.

Why?

Because they are sinners.

What?

We'll talk about that more later.

Children With Jesus

To Know My Jesus

Two things about my Jesus,
I want to comprehend,
To know Him as well
as I do my closest friend.
To understand His love
in a very special way.
To know Him in my life,
to walk with Him each day.
I want to see His outstretched hand
extended lovingly.
I want to feel His arms
wrapped securely around me.
I want to hear His Spirit.
His wisdom to impart.
I want to know my Jesus,
His love within my heart.

> Jesus called for the little ones, saying,
> "Allow the children to come to Me,
> and do not forbid them,
> for the kingdom of God belongs to such as these.
> Truly I say to you,
> whoever does not receive the kingdom of God
> like a child will not enter it at all."
>
> Luke 18:16,17 (NASB)

1997

Journal Entry

Father, I need to hear from You about going to church this morning. While I was in bed it seemed You said to stay home and spend time with You. My first response was—But Lord, You know I like people and want to see people today! Besides, what about apologizing to Laura and Phyllis for being demanding? I can't do that from home.

What about Josh? What kind of example am I setting for him? What about Steve? If I stay home he's likely to stay home also. I want to force him to go. He's whining about his body being sore.

Please forgive me, Lord, for struggling so much with You leading me to stay home this morning. Please forgive my lack of trust in You. Why is this issue of what church people think of me so huge in my life? Remember how You worked with me on that in our last prayer session? My mother's issues with church. I forgave her, church people, and myself, and yet, it's still here. Maybe this issue is so big we'll have to work on it in pieces. Only You know, Lord.

Irritable this morning. Distracted by Steve's noises, etc. So spoiled during weekdays to have these quiet mornings with You, Jesus. I love You, Jesus! Please hold me today. I feel like crying this morning.

Oh, Jesus, You are so great and wise and I am so small and unwise, yet I struggle on–desperately wrestling for control. Do other people fight You so hard, Lord? I surrender my will to you and then–to my dismay–I realize I'm trying to control again. Will I ever learn? Maybe this is what the apostle Paul meant when he said: "I don't understand what I do. For I don't do what I want to do; but do what I hate instead." (Romans 7:15 my paraphrase)

Wow, Lord! You were right. We do have so much work to do together this morning. Thank You for Your Holy Spirit, Father.

My Lord admonished me to forgive friends for not being available when I needed them. Confessed and repented of my sin of demanding them to meet my needs. Now waiting on the Lord to confirm my need to confess and apologize to friends and to provide a time and place for such. Also, need to know how to do so graciously.

Annie hasn't been out to play very much in the past two weeks. Still, we continue our dialogue concerning food–so we are constantly in touch. She doesn't want to take the rap if someone else is overeating or making unwise choices. She quickly tells me "I'm not doing this, Mama" or "It has so much yucky fat, Mama."

She has had to do without hamburgers a few times because I didn't have any money. I try to make it up to her by doing other things for her with things I have on hand. Not sure if she understands about the money, but she never complains or begs. She just gets quiet.

I know! When we don't have money we could send her to Jesus for a big juicy delicious hamburger from His banquet table. It's certainly worth a try! As I mention it she says, *Yum.*

I hate having no money. Yes, my Lord is my provider and the lifter of my head, but I hate being poor. Steve and I have been coming against the spirit and bondage of poverty in the name of Jesus.

The other day after we priced a little satin pillow to put in the casket for Steve's dad we both said, "Being poor sucks!" We probably would have made an emotional decision if we had money anyway. Spend far too much on flowers that would end up in decay. But still, we wished we could have been able to do more.

We bought a single long-stemmed rose to put in his hand. That ended up costing $7.00. The money was designated for gas, but I was in so much grief I was determined we contribute something. No matter how small.

So, Jesus, how is Annie and where is she with You?

She must first accept Me. Then she can learn to forgive.

Annie. Annie. Where are you?

Giggle.

Are you hiding?

BOO!

I see you! Were you behind me?

Yes. Mama, where's the baby?

I'll go get her.

Mama, the baby needs a hat.

She does?

Yes. Her head is cold.

Okay, we'll get her a hat.

And clothes?

And clothes. Maybe at Thrift Town.

What about Aunt Vivie? Think she might have something? Aunt Vivie, Aunt Vivie, Aunt Vivie...

Well, we surely can ask. Annie, when Josh is home I need to pay attention to him. Do you understand?

Why?

Well, you and Josh need to share me, and you get to be with me almost all the time. Josh doesn't.

He hurts the baby doll.

Yes. It's because he is jealous and he thinks it's a little weird for his mama to carry a baby doll around.

It's not weird.

I know, and you know, but he doesn't know.

The baby is cold.

I'll hold her close until I can find a blankie, okay? Let's go look for a blankie.

So now the baby is all wrapped up in Josh's baby blanket. The big teddy bear is babysitting so I can either play the piano or get dressed. It's 12:40 so the guys will be home from church soon.

Time for evening church service–very upsetting.

"You're probably upset because we were running late. Let's skip choir today," offers Steve.

Time is not the problem. This is an issue of church attendance.

"I can't find my shoes. Has anyone seen my shoes?" hollers Josh.

As much as I hate to, we have to face this.

I will work with you during the service.

Clutching Steve's hand. I don't know the first song.

Notice how difficult it is to see any individual choir member? No one on the platform is looking at you in particular when you are up there.

What a relief! When I close my eyes I can focus on You. It's nice to take my attention off myself.

"Hi, Viv. Is it too late to call?"

"The children are in bed so your timing's perfect."

"I was wondering if you'd pray with me to ask the Holy Spirit to show me why I have such a phobia of attending church."

"Sure."

"Father, I know the church is Your body and if we love You we have fellowship with other believers. I want fellowship. I need fellowship. I want to worship You with others who love You. But for some reason, I have a real problem with church and I can't figure out why on my own. I know it's not because of the people at Bethesda. They've been supportive in so many ways. Please show me why I have such a phobia of attending church services.

"I see people who attended my daddy's church when I was young. I can see they love one another. I see the homely little wood and cinder block building. I'm overcome with shame related to Daddy's control of members. Shame for Daddy putting himself on God's level.

"I forgive you Daddy for embarrassing me. For controlling your parishioners, and for elevating yourself as a god.

"Father, forgive me for being ashamed of my daddy. Forgive me for accepting shame that was not even my own.

"'No one comes here for you. They come to worship Me.'"

I become slightly distracted by beautiful classical guitar music playing in the background. "Is Stan playing his guitar?"

"Yes."

"What is he playing?"

"He says it's called 'The Cathedral.'"

"No way! Does he know what we're praying about right now?"

"No."

"Wow!"

We resume as I hear Jesus speak. "'When you come to worship you don't have to do anything. You don't have to minister or sing to bless anyone. You are there only to worship Me. It's a time set aside for Me to be with My bride. Are you ready to greet your brothers and sisters?'

"May I have Your guidance with each person I speak to or shake hands with?"

Yes.

"Okay.

"Jesus takes my hand and leads me through the doors.

"Hello, Mrs. Baker. I want to forgive and ask your forgiveness..." One by one, every member is greeted with forgiveness, love, and acceptance.

"I forgive my mother for blaming me for nearly killing her when I was born. I'm sorry Mother you almost died. I forgive myself for causing you so much fear and pain. Jesus, I give You all of my shame and guilt associated with Mom's health."

Journal Entry

Your mother beat you as an infant.

That's disgusting! I can't believe such an atrocity! Where were You, God?

I saved your life. Yes, I was there and I saved your life because I have a plan for you. Your mother was emotionally unstable. She was very imbalanced hormonally, chemically, and spiritually.

Remember how tiny you were at four pounds and ten ounces? Doctors told her you were too small to suckle enough to produce milk. She cried many tears because she wanted so much to nurse you. She was away from her mother. She had no support from anyone who could help her with breastfeeding and she was too timid to ask. This compounded feelings of inadequacy. She did not know Me well enough to draw strength from Me–to invite Me to help her. Your father tried to stand in the gap...

Father, I forgive my mother for beating me as an infant. I forgive my mother for beating me as a child. Father, I forgive You for allowing it to happen and I give You my current feelings of disgust over this issue.

Lord, forgive me. I have sinned all these years by judging my mother so cruelly–so harshly.

Read My Word—Psalm 34.

That's my favorite Psalm.

I know. Smiling. There's a divine reason for that.

> Those who look to Him are radiant; their faces are never covered with shame.
> – Psalm 34:5 (NASB)

Nurture the baby doll as though it were you as an infant in this quiet place I have for you and Me. It will bring healing to your soul.

My, how realistic-looking this doll is! I wonder how old I was when I was this size. Certainly not when I was a newborn. Josh was pretty big, so size is irrelevant. Sitting with the doll on my lap, wrapped in Josh's blankie, gently stroking its face and head.

Thank You, Father, for I would never have known about the need for this healing. How could I ever remember anything that far back? Thank You, Lord. Thank You, Jesus.

Rock the baby. Sing to the baby.

"Hi, Faith. Come on in." Viv gives me a big hug. "The children are watching T.V. We can pray in my room."

"Okay. Do you think we could call Paul to share our victories and ask for prayer for Annie?"

"Sure." Usual greetings follow with Paul.

"Did Vivien tell you about when she first called me about your situation?" Paul asks.

"She said you were helping her, but that's about all."

"It was midnight here when she called. I had been reading a book by Neil Anderson. I had just finished reading a paragraph about multiple personalities. He recommends helping them find healing by leading each personality to Christ."

"Wow! Talk about timing! It's working, too!"

Paul prays for us before leaving. "Father, we praise You for the work You're doing in Faith's life. You are such an awesome God. Please continue Your work tonight. Please reveal what Annie needs to set her free from her pain. In Jesus' name, amen."

"Thank you, Paul."

"Any time. Bye."

"Annie," Vivien says, "will you come out and talk to me?" Long pause.

"Hi, Vivie."

"Hi, Annie. Have you been playing with Jesus?"

"Sometimes–in the playroom and outside on the teeter-totter. He's playing and laughing now. His laughter fills the house."

"What's the difference between playing on the inside and on the outside?"

"I don't know. I don't know how to say it, but it feels good to get to come out and be known as Annie and play like I want to. I don't like Mama's big body, though. I wish I could sit on your lap, but this body is too big. I might squash you like a pancake."

"It's like a prison, isn't it?"

"Yes."

"Do you want to be set free?"

"You know it!"

"Let's ask God how you can be set free. Okay?"

"Okay."

"Father in heaven, please show Annie what will make her free. Show her what she needs to forgive to be set free from

Faith's grown-up body." She opens her eyes and lifts her head. "Annie, where's Jesus?"

"Right over there," pointing.

"When God made everything He made people to love Him and walk with Him the way you get to be with Jesus in the nursery."

"Really? Like here in the system—only on the outside?"

"Yes. But God didn't want to force His children to be with Him. He wanted them to want to be with Him because they love Him. The way you like to be with your mama all the time.

"So He put a tree in the middle of a garden. He told Adam and Eve—the first man and woman—not to eat the fruit on the tree so they would have a choice to obey or not. He also made a lot of other fruit trees for them to eat from so they wouldn't feel like they had to do without good food.

"He didn't tell them that disobeying would cause a lot of problems for people. He told them the worst thing that would happen if they disobeyed. If they ate the fruit they would die.

"Well, the fruit looked really good. Satan told Eve that eating the fruit would make her as smart as God, so she ate some and gave some to Adam. Disobeying is called sin and it separated Adam and Eve and all the people after them from God."

"God must have cried."

"He probably did. But God knew they would disobey, so He had a plan to send Jesus to bring people back to Him again.

"Sin is being selfish. It's thinking only of what we want—not caring what God or other people want."

"I'm selfish."

"God wants us to love Him and other people so we won't be selfish."

"I don't know how to love."

"No one knows how to really love since sin came into the world. That's why people hurt other people. We need Jesus to help us love the way He does. Jesus wants to heal you from all the pain that people gave you. He wants to set you free so you won't hurt anymore."

"There's never been a time when I didn't hurt."

"That's because you were created out of pain."

"I don't know about that. I'm 'lergic to pain."

"Let's pray and ask Jesus why you hurt so He can heal it."

"Okay."

"Jesus, please show Annie why she hurts so much." A moment of silence.

"Ooh! I'm locked in a closet. Where's Jesus? I'm scared and it's too dark to see Him. Vivie, will you pray and ask Jesus where He is?"

"Jesus is the light so He will chase away all the darkness."

"Yes. I see Him now. He says He's going to shine His light in every closet every time I'm locked in one! Jesus says my mother locked me up to protect me from herself. Wow! I thought she didn't love me, but she must have because she protected me."

"You need to forgive your mother for locking you in the closet."

"No. I don't want to."

"You don't have to want to but you have to forgive her to be free. Forgiving your mother will set you free from the closet forever."

"Really? How?"

"Because bitterness and anger are the locks to the closet door. Forgiveness is the key to unlocking it. You can ask Jesus to help you forgive if you want to."

"Jesus, will you help me forgive her?" Pause. "I forgive you, Mother, for locking me in the closet."

"Good! You did it!"

"Yeah! Now I remember that Mother wouldn't let me eat because she said I was too fat."

"Are you ready to forgive her for depriving you of food and for neglecting you?"

"I forgive you, Mother, for not letting me eat and for calling me fat. ...Jesus is reminding me someone left some crackers out for me to find. I would hide them in the closet so I'd have them when I needed them."

"Who gave you the crackers?"

"Jesus did. Jesus has His hand out with a spoon in it. There's love on the spoon. Wow! Love has a taste!"

"How does it taste?"

"Good! I can't say what it's like, but it makes me feel full, like Maymee felt when she came home from the concert."

"Jesus shared His last meal with His friends before He died. He told His friends He was going to die soon. He told them to eat bread to remember His body when He was gone. He told them to drink wine to remember His blood that was shed on the cross. When we do that, we call it communion."

"Yeah! Jesus is having communion with me. Right here in the closet with the crackers! Just Jesus and me. Wow!"

"Jesus said, 'I am the Bread of Life and Living Waters. Follow Me and you will never be thirsty again'"

"Wow! The light surrounding me is Jesus giving me a big hug! Jesus says He is in the closet protecting me. The closet isn't a scary place–it's a safe place.

"Mother locked me in an old 'fridge-rater. Why did you want to kill me, Mother? I was only a little girl! ...Jesus says she didn't want to kill me, only scare me."

"Are you ready to forgive her?"

"Not really, but I forgive you, Mother, for locking me in the 'fridge-rater.

"I forgive the debt of locking me in the refrigerator." I, Faith, say. "Jesus, I give You my terror, anxiety, claustrophobia, and panic attacks. I forgive you, Mother, for making me wear dirty clothes. And for keeping me dirty unless we went to church or somewhere. I give the debt and surrender rejection, neglect, and worthlessness to You, Jesus."

"Jesus wants to wash you as white as snow," Vivien says.

"I like that! Jesus wears bright white clothes. They sure are clean."

"Would you like to see yourself?"

"Of course!" A moment passes. "I'm wearing a beautiful white ruffled dress. It's spotless and my hair is squeaky clean and shiny!"

Journal Entry

Prayed for Annie at Viv's tonight. Took about an hour and a half.

Prayed over many issues–locked in closets, refrigerator, and much more. Jesus showed up and really blessed the session. We prayed until we no longer heard any new issues revealed by the Holy Spirit.

The most amazing thing happened! After forgiving the final debt, we noticed Annie's high-pitched girly voice faded out. Faith's more mature voice was the one praying. We both realized it almost at the same time. Viv was the one brave enough to ask our question out loud. Had Annie integrated right there in the prayer session?

I dare not ask, I thought I was whole once or twice before. Decided to hold such a possibility in my heart and think on it. Wow! Wouldn't it be even more fantastic than anything else He's done?

"Hi, Faith. Sit down. How have you been?"

"Hi, Dr. Kathy. God is doing some fantastic things through my prayer sessions with Vivien. Things are going fast with the Holy Spirit guiding us."

"That's great. I'm excited for you."

"I feel like Nathan needs some help now. He's wanting to come to the front."

"That's fine. Nathan, what is your purpose for the system?"

"My purpose is to carry out the wishes of the system. If the system wants to live–I'll guarantee safety. If the system wants to die–I'll guarantee the success of that option."

"Would you consider changing the suicide option to adding on a nurturing room to the safe house? The others can go there to begin to receive healing from Jesus."

"I'll have to think it over. I have to know I can trust this Jesus guy."

"Jesus wouldn't want to take your role from you, but be a co-worker alongside you. I've known Him for a long time. He is of impeccable character."

"Dr. Kathy, I think Nathan will probably have to spend some time with Jesus. They're probably getting to know each other right now in the gym. I think Nathan will be impressed with how well Jesus can pump iron."

"I imagine he will."

Journal Entry – a.m.

Jesus and Nathan are working together, adding extra rooms onto the safe house for people who need respite. Jesus' muscular arms are visible under white tee shirt sleeves. He's wearing jeans, a tool belt around His waist, and a ball cap on His head. Nathan is sizing Him up–making sure He can be trusted.

Annie has a system all her own, a nursery full of children with a door she refuses to open for anybody. Jesus talks to her. *I already know who's in your nursery. You can trust Me. Will you open the door?*

Hesitating, she finally opens the door. Hand in hand with Mama Faith on one side and Jesus on the other, Annie leads them into her system. It's dark at first, but the light of Jesus begins to shine. Several children peek out, afraid to make a sound.

It's okay, Annie encourages, *Jesus is my friend and I know you can trust Him!* She climbs on His lap to show she likes Him.

A timid child steps forward. *Monica.* Her eyes widen with surprise that Jesus knows her name. *I've come to take away your pain.* Taking her on His lap He whispers in her ear the very incident of abuse that happened to cause her split. Sobbing, she clings to Him. *Do you want the pain to go away?*

Oh yes!

Jesus stands in the gap for the mother who committed the abuse. *Please forgive me!*

This deeply moves Monica. *Yes, I forgive her!*

Hundreds of dirty foul-smelling children with tangled hair hide behind large rocks. These are the children who once dwelt in the scary mansion I blew up over a year ago. They gradually creep out.

Jesus gives undivided attention to each child. He helps them walk through each incident, emotion, and the process of forgiving. He makes it simple for them so they understand and believe Him. There are hundreds of children–maybe more, but Jesus is in no hurry. No matter how many children there are, Jesus remains until everyone is healed.

You must all join together to become Annie so you can fight against any of the issues we dealt with today. You can stand against it in My name.

I dial the phone for Annie. "Hi, Vivie."

"Hi, Annie. What are you up to today?"

"I'm spending time with Jesus."

"Really? Cool."

"Jesus healed all the children in my world and now they're all gone. I'm the only one left. I've been playing in a meadow with Jesus. We have necklaces of flowers on our heads and necks."

"That sounds really nice. I bet you look beautiful with your flowers."

"Uh-huh."

"Annie, how would you like to be a butterfly? I think it may be your time to fly like a beautiful butterfly."

"Mama doesn't want me to go."

"I see. Do you suppose we should pray for Faith?"

"Okay."

"Father, thank You for healing all the children in Annie's world, and thank You for healing Annie. Please give Faith the courage to commit Annie to You. Please fill the void Annie might leave with Your presence and Your love."

"Father, I realize Annie has been my constant little companion. We've been having ongoing conversations for so long, especially concerning food issues. I guess I hoped she would conquer that compulsive eating behavior for me.

"I realize it's wrong not to let Annie go. Please give me the strength to release her to You." Sorrow fills my heart and flows from my eyes. "Jesus, I give Annie to You to integrate into me. I release the debt of never having more children–especially the little girl I've always wanted. I forgive myself, and I forgive Steve for agreeing to stop at one child. Lord, I forgive You for not giving me a daughter. Forgive me for resenting You for that..."

"...Father, who can we pray for now? Do you want to continue Your work with Annie, or should we pray for Maymee? Please bring me to the place I need to be so I can allow You to work in me."

I close my eyes and listen for the Lord. "The Holy Spirit is telling me we need to pray for Janet. He's telling me to introduce her to the system."

Brief silence. "Janet, this is Vivien."

"Hello, Janet."

A quiet sad, "Hi."

"Janet, I'm Faith's friend. We want to pray for you so you won't hurt anymore. Would you like that?"

"Yeah."

"Before we pray, I would like to invite Jesus to be with us. He's the One who will take your pain away. Would you like to meet Him?"

"Yeah."

"Jesus, we invite You to come guide our session and to be with Janet now." Silence.

"Do you see Him?"

"I see a man with a bunch of sheep. He's carrying a long stick as tall as He is."

"That's Jesus. He's the Good Shepherd. He's very kind and gentle. He loves all His sheep very much and takes good care of them. Did you know that sheep are very timid animals?"

"No."

"They are. Sheep are afraid of everyone and everything. They don't trust anyone except their Master and only then if their Master is good to them."

"Really? I can't trust anyone, either."

"Do you see how His sheep trust Him? You can trust Jesus, too. He's God's Son, and He's never done anything to hurt anyone. He never will, either, because He is love. He loves His sheep so much that He gave His own life to protect them."

"There's a whole bunch of other kids here, too. Some of them are my age. Some are younger. They're all around the Shepherd. He's hugging them and letting them climb all over Him."

"How old are you?"

"Ten."

"Those children are Jesus' sheep."

"Really? How? They look like kids to me."

"Jesus loves each of those children like a Shepherd who loves and protects His sheep. Janet, I would like to pray for you now, but I need to know what to pray for. Would you please tell me what I can pray for you?"

"I don't want to. It hurts too much."

"I know it does. I'm really sorry that you're in such pain. That's why I would like to help you, but we need to know exactly what to pray for."

"Grandpa did something that hurt me. It hurts a lot."

"I'm very sorry, Janet. Do you want to tell me what he did?"

"No. It hurts too much to talk about it. Jesus says I'm resisting Him. I'm resisting facing the memory."

"Viv, I know what memory she's thinking of. I think she experienced sexual abuse when she was younger. It happened during the one or two times when Grandpa came to visit. I don't think Grandma came with him. I think she'll integrate quickly if she faces it, but she's resisting."

"How did I know it was wrong? Because I feel bad about it?"

"That's the confusing part," Vivien replies. "When someone you love and admire does something bad to you it's hard to know if it's acceptable or not. But you feel bad about it either way."

"Yeah, he was Grandpa. He chewed tobacco. That's disgusting, but as long as you don't step in it or get in the way of his spitting you learn to live with it."

"Yes. It's something like that."

I don't want to cry about it anymore. I'm so tired of crying about it.

"Since you don't want to talk about it, why don't you just tell Jesus what happened," Vivien suggests.

"I thought He already knew." A moment of silent talking to Jesus. "Why did You let him do that? Why didn't You knock my grandpa upside the head?"

"That's the problem with sin. It hurts everyone. Even innocent children. But it allows us to experience God more intimately through healing than we would if we're happy all the time. Wounds in life can make us stronger when we overcome trauma. It also makes us more sympathetic to other hurting people. Jesus can wash away all the shame and pain of your past if you want Him to."

"I do! The Good Shepherd is nice."

"The Good Shepherd loves you as He loves His special little lamb."

"I know, He's telling me I can be one of His lambs."

"Would you like to be one of His lambs?"

"Yeah."

"All you have to do is ask."

"How?"

"Just say, Jesus, will you be my Good Shepherd?"

"Okay. Jesus, will You be my Good Shepherd?" A small smile. "He says okay. He's showing me how safe He keeps His lambs. He says He'll carry me. And when He doesn't carry me He'll leave me in the safety of His flock. He is very nice, but I'll wait and see...He wants me to go for a walk with Him. Is that okay?"

"Yes. That'll be great."

"Are you sure it'll be okay?"

"Yes. He will never hurt you. It'll give you the chance to get to know Him."

"Will we come back?"

"Yes, you will."

"Okay. Bye."

"Viv, I feel the Holy Spirit prompting me to forgive my mother."

"Okay."

Several silent moments. "I can't. It hurts too much. The pain is too raw."

"You don't have to feel like forgiving. Let's pray and ask God to help you."

"Father, I can't do it on my own. Please help me forgive."

After a moment of silence, I relent. "…I forgive you, Mother, for belittling me. I forgive you for transferring your feelings of incompetence, fear, fear of rejection, and worthlessness to me. I forgive you for transferring your negative spirit to me.

"I'm sorry that you never liked me, and I forgive you for that. I forgive you for telling me I'd never amount to anything and that I never finished anything. For controlling me in church and making me your puppet…"

And so it goes until the session is complete.

Total Integration

You Are My Life

Groping in darkness, I could not see,
Blinded by pain life has dealt me.
Desperation settled over my soul,
Ending it all was within my control.
Life was so loud I could not see
God and His love were there for me.

Then as I wavered a Light became song
Guiding my steps to where I belong.
Jesus, You are my Light in this darkness called life.
You shine on me when my world is all strife.
You wrap me in love I'd only dreamed of.
You are my Light, Lord, You are my Love.

How blessed is he whose wrongdoing is forgiven,
Whose sin is covered!
How blessed is a person whose guilt
The LORD does not take into account,
And in whose spirit there is no deceit!

When I kept silent about my sin, my body wasted away
Through my groaning all day long.
For day and night Your hand was heavy upon me;
My vitality failed as with the dry heat of summer.
I acknowledged my sin to You,
And I did not hide my guilt;
I said, "I will confess my wrongdoings to the LORD;"
And You forgave the guilt of my sin.

Psalm 32:1-5 (NASB)

1997

Journal Entry

Father, I feel a little disoriented or something this morning. Please let me be in tune with You. I need You, Jesus. I want to do what You would have me do today.

In the name of Jesus, I command you, Satan, to go. Get out of here selfishness, vain glory, and confusion. In the name of Jesus, you must leave!

Father, give me the mind of Christ. I need Your thoughts today, Your cohesiveness. My thoughts are scattering quite a bit, jumping around a lot. Why is it after every new victory there seems to be a new attack from Satan? It seems with each step of higher ground we gain he's determined to pull us back down or hinder us from progressing.

Well, Devil, not today! In the name and through the blood of Jesus you have to go.

Father, I need a hedge of protection around me physically and around my mind. Please let Your armor protect me this day. Let me continue to take up the sword of truth and use it today, Jesus. Lord, please direct my steps.

Read My Word–Romans chapters four and five.

> Therefore, since we have been justified through faith, we have peace with God through whom we have gained access by faith into this grace in which we now stand. And we boast in the hope of the glory of God. Not only so, but we also glory in our sufferings, because we know that suffering produces perseverance, perseverance, character, and character, hope. And hope does not put us to shame, because God's love has been poured out into our hearts through the Holy Spirit, who has been given to us.
> – Romans 5:1-5 (NIV)

While reading the Word, about all at once in unison, Maymee and Nathan integrated! It happened very quickly and smoothly by the power of the Holy Spirit. It was like I had no part in it at all. I simply became aware of it.

Nathan evidently came to trust Jesus and His ability to protect anyone in the system. To give them a safe place to be when they couldn't make it on their own. Since he was created to be our protector, he had no pain to deal with, so he integrated.

Maymee told me yesterday I didn't need her anymore. She said Jesus was more than able to continue His healing in me. I must admit that I didn't want to release Maymee. Maybe I'll recognize some of her traits in myself eventually.

Goodbye, Maymee. You helped the people in the system a lot with your encouragement and knowledge of God. Hey girl, I know you're a part of me now, but I am sad that I can no longer call you out or let you be in the front.

Jesus, please put Your hand on my heart and mind today.

> Mother's debts forgiven by Maymee:
> – beaten with a rod
> – threatened abandonment
> – threatened to get us a black mama

So, Lord Jesus, I forgive these debts as I speak them out loud. I forgive my mother and my daddy. I give you all my feelings and memories related to these debts. Please wash them in Your blood.

Hallelujah! Jesus is working in me–with me. He still hasn't given up on me! Thank You, Jesus!

Journal Entry

Happy Valentine's Day! Will You be my Valentine, Jesus? I love You, Lord! Thank You for Steve's new job at Motorola! You are so good, Jesus–my provider.

"Hi, Viv. Are the kids in bed yet?"

"Hello, Faith. Yes, and I'm ready to pray. Who are we going to pray for tonight?"

"Let's pray for Joey. He's been pretty rebellious lately. He has a lot of anger. He wants to smoke and drink."

"Okay, let's ask God what's going on with Joey.

"Father, I can see Joey is angry. I lift him up to You and ask You to reveal why he's angry and what can be done about it. In Jesus' name, amen.

"Joey, will you talk with me?"

"Sure. Why not?"

"Why do you want to smoke and drink?"

"To get back at the mother. I'm miffed at the way she treated all of us and everyone in the system is letting her off the hook lately."

"Those who have forgiven your mother have been healed from their pain. Would you like to be free from your pain?"

"Yeah, but I don't want to forgive the mother. I hate her."

"Hate is like super glue that bonds you to those you hate. Jesus said that being kind to your enemies is like heaping coals of fire on their heads."

"I like the sound of that."

"May I pray with you?"

"I guess so."

"Father, please show Joey how to forgive his mother."

"Viv, I see Joey at the foot of the cross. He needs to take his sin, anger, and forgiveness and nail it to the cross as he comes to know Jesus. I believe that's the direction Jesus wants to go with Joey. I think we're supposed to read about the cross in the Word as Jesus and Joey walk the Via Dolorosa. I'm going to go read my Bible, okay?"

"Okay. Bye, Faith. Bye, Joey."

"Bye.

"Bye."

Journal Entry

Wow! Thank You, Holy Spirit for showing us so quickly what Joey needed during our telephone prayer session tonight!

Read the account of the crucifixion in Luke.

Joey is beginning to realize who Jesus really is. He has a gold headband around His forehead and is wearing a white shirt, jeans, and boots. It's a clear contrast to Joey's black headband, clothes, and fingerless gloves. Jesus is revealing to Joey that He is the TOUGHEST dude around! Jesus, Joey, and a band of angels are riding–Harleys?

Please forgive me, Lord, if this is in any way disrespectful to You–but I see Jesus riding a Harley alongside Joey!

Oh, Father, thank You for Your love and for not turning a deaf ear to me.

I feel discouraged. Dr. Kathy doesn't completely attribute my inner healing to the work the Holy Spirit's been doing in me. Only by Your Spirit could this final chapter in my healing be complete. You are the only One who knows me well enough to direct the inner healing and forgiving process.

I'm confused. Yes, therapy with Dr. Kathy has been of great value to our entire family and me these past eight years. I continue to benefit from our sessions. But since Vivien and I began intensive prayer sessions the results have been phenomenal!

As I have forgiven each debt and debtor–sometimes only with the Holy Spirit's grace and help–there's been closure. Healing–a finished product–like I've never had in therapy. I've felt light as a feather. Like some big baggage has been lifted off my back. It has been quite a journey. Dr. Kathy says all the years in therapy have equipped me to get in tune inside and allow God to work. I don't know. She may be right.

I don't know the mind of God. He certainly has used Dr. Kathy and other doctors and therapists in my healing journey. They taught me and nudged me toward facing my monsters. It's also true that this is the time for my healing as He has so vividly shown of late. Yes, I've been willing and obedient, but it was He who put the desire in my heart and the drive to stick with it day in and day out. He also gave me Vivien, who wouldn't let go of her role as a prayer warrior, and gently nudged me when I resisted.

Thank You, God! You're my Counselor, my Prince of Peace. You are my sanity. You're my health and the air I breathe! I give You this day and my life today as I spend time with Josh. Lord, I give You Josh–let him see You in me. Please direct my steps.

Jesus is riding motorcycles with Joey and has added to His safe house a garage to work on the cycles. Joey is amazed at how much Jesus knows about him–his likes, etc.

Hey, Jesus. Are You really God?

What do YOU think?

C'mon now–don't mess around with my head–Ya know–cuz she does that with me. Maybe she told you what I'm like.

I know all about you, Joey–why you're here inside of Faith. I know your pain. I want to help you.

I'm not worth it, Man. Go help somebody else.

Do you truly want Me to do that? Silence. It's one day at a time, you know. Remember the 12-step program for addictions–taking one day at a time? I'm the God you trust to take You through each day.

I can't do it yet.

It's your choice, Joey. I can't force you.

Really? But you're God.

Yes, but I didn't create robots.

She's afraid for me to talk.

I know, but Faith knows I'm with her.

Yeah.

Why don't you show Me that motor you want us to work on?

Yeah, but no funny stuff. I want us to do this legit.

There's hope for you yet! Smiling.

Know what? I'm all the times she wishes she would have screamed or hit back. I'm all the times she wanted to run away. I'm the angry one. I helped her rebel-escape, smoke pot and drink booze-just in her head-but we just escaped. She's having a hard time letting me go, too. I was her imaginary tough guy. I'm only real to me and to her, Ya know?

Pausing to think. I've seen what You've done for the others-I believe in You. You're one tough dude! What You did on the cross. Man, I could never do that! So, what do I do, Man?

Just ask Me.

That's all? Jesus, will You come into my life?

Yes, Joey. I'm glad you've invited Me in.

Now I know I have the best sponsor!

Let's ride!

"Hey, Viv."

"Hey, Faith. What's up?"

"God's been dealing with Joey! Joey confessed his rebellion and stuff. Then he asked Jesus into his heart."

"Wow! Great!"

"We're ready to pray if you are."

"You bet. Father, please show Joey all he needs to give to You."

"I'm lugging a great big bag. It's really heavy."

"That bag contains the burden of hate. Why don't you open it and show us what's inside."

"I hate the mother for not helping us make it to the bathroom when we wore braces. I desperately wanted to hurt her for that."

"Are you ready to start emptying the bag so you won't be burdened with it anymore?"

"Yeah."

"The only way to do that is to forgive every debt and debtor in that bag."

"Yeah, I know...I forgive the mother for not helping us to the bathroom when we wore braces. Jesus, forgive me for hating the parents and for all the horrible things I wanted to do like hit, cut, and kill them. I forgive myself for hating and wanting to hurt them. I accept God's forgiveness."

"Joey, you no longer need to be a negative part of Faith. I can give you a new assignment. I give you boots of peace."

"Cool. I forgive the parents for giving our brother special treatment. Jesus, please forgive me for being jealous of him and for treating him so badly–for slapping him."

"Forgive yourself for those things."

"I forgive myself...Faith, will you forgive me for shouting at you to do what I wanted?

"I forgive you.

"Jesus, I give You my addictions and obsessive behavior. Lord, I confess I haven't wanted to let go of my addictions because I wouldn't have an excuse for my actions. I give my obsessions and compulsive behavior to You. Please forgive me for this...

"Viv, we don't see anything else in the bag now. It's pretty light."

"Father, thank You for Your mercy that enables us to come to Your throne of grace to lay our sins before You. Thank You for Your faithfulness to forgive every sin, sinner, and misdirected anger and accusation against You. Thank You specifically for extending Your grace to Joey and Faith. You truly are a mighty God.

"Father, I pray Your love will fill Joey's bag to overflowing. Let Your love spill out over the bag like a great balloon–bringing light all around Joey."

"The bag is still dark inside, Viv. I think there must be something remaining. Father, please show me what is left that's preventing Your love to fill the bag. I come against rebellion in the name of Jesus. Please, Lord, forgive me for my rebellion. In the name of Jesus, I rebuke the spirit of homicide and suicide. You must go. I also come against the spirit of profanity in the name of Jesus.

"Father, is there anything else You want me to work on with Joey? Please show me. What is it I feel still needs to be covered?"

"Release him for yourself, Faith," Vivien says.

"Please forgive me, Lord, for wanting to hold on to Joey–even though he accepted You! I know You want to make me whole. Please make me obedient to Your voice. In the name of Jesus, I release Joey–only by the power of the Holy Spirit."

Joey, Jesus, and a gang of angels ride.

"I love You, Jesus."

Journal Entry

Holy Spirit, please reveal where Janet is in the system. Let me hear Your voice about what You want to do with her.

Janet is shaking–from the cold?

No. From fear.

Fear of what?

Fear of falling.

Physical falling or figuratively?

Both.

She's on the edge of a cliff. She is afraid. The Good Shepherd is just an arm's reach away, reaching out to her, calling to her.

Janet.

She's nearly blinded with fear. She is weak. Wind is blowing fiercely around them like a storm blowing in. The reason Janet is in the system is because Faith had to be perfect.

Why a personality just for THIS, Lord? Haven't we covered this already?

I will show you.

Why would she need You as the Good Shepherd?

Patience, My child.

Sorry, Lord.

Janet helped you when things were unbearable in the area of perfectionism.

Didn't Daphne handle that?

Only partly. She handled the performance aspect. Janet handles the rest.

So what else do I need to know or do, now, Lord?

Back to the cliff. Janet.

She reaches out for Him. *Jesus, help me!* Instantly she is in His arms. They are off the cliff and out of danger. Jesus draws her near as she shivers. He wraps His cloak around her.

I'm sorry I wandered away, she whispers.

I forgive you.

I want to stay with You forever. Can I? He hugs her.

Now Father, please reveal debts needing to be forgiven and the sins needing confession. One by one I repeat the tedious steps of forgiveness.

Mother's Debts:
– yanking my hair with a comb
– screaming at me for accidentally breaking dishes

I release fear, anxiety, helplessness, and hopelessness.

Parents' Debts:
– not being allowed normal feelings
– harshly rebuked for brushing cracker crumbs off my hands onto the floor

I release feelings of inadequacy, failure, anger, confusion, and anxiety.

The kitchen in that big old house. I keep picturing the kitchen. Much of the abuse happened at that house. So many debts to forgive–like clearing out a bank account or vault. So many feelings to give to the Lord. Feelings that include failure, discouragement, and inferiority.

Oh, Jesus, it hurts! I really tried to be what they wanted. I messed up–yes, even sinned–but it hurts. Please heal the pain. Show me now, Father, who I am in You. I need You to be my Anchor. As all my people integrate I feel a little shaky about how I'll handle things when tempted to dissociate. My Hope is in You.

I give you Joey and Janet now if they're ready. Your timing is always best, Lord! Thank You. Thank You. Thank You!

Journal Entry

Last night I prayed with Viv for what we think may have been the last of the inner healing. Healing the people inside of me! Rejoiced over what the Lord has done. Asked Him to reveal any other darkness needing to be dealt with. Ended up praising Him. Thanking Him. Loving Him.

Would like to share with the group about the integration.

Father, I give myself to You today. My brand new self thanking You for being my rock, my anchor, my super glue. Thank You for my health–for feeling well today. Praise You. Thank You for food, clothing, and shelter. Thank You for keeping us all in Your hand. Please continue to direct my day, Holy Spirit.

Journal Entry

Thank You, Lord, for the new song. Time with You on the piano was special. Forgive me, Lord, I slept in longer than I should have. Could have spent more time with You.

Lord, I feel like I'm just waking up to realize I'm a forty-one-year-old woman. One who's been married for almost seventeen years and has a twelve-year-old son. Wow! My life has been a blur.

Thank You for being my rock, my sanity. For holding me all this time in Your hand. You are the God of the Ages. You care for all Your children, individually, personally. Oh, Jesus, You are Lord.

Thank You for Your blood covering my sins. Thank You for making me emotionally and mentally well. I've never felt better. Let me walk with You now–out in the world, too. Life was so much easier when I was closed up with You at home all day. It was quiet with no distractions.

Journal Entry

Father, this week has been PMS week. Felt a little nervous and quick-tempered. Need wisdom on when to set boundaries with Josh and when to stop and give him lots of hugs. I think he and Steve need more love from me than I could ever give. They need Your love more than mine. Please love them through me, Father.

Being a single personality has brought quietness to my mind and life. Sometimes I wonder who I am now. Wondering which personality turned out to be the strongest part of me.

Each person was healed by accepting responsibility for their actions and making Jesus the Lord of their lives. But I am human–as were they–so the capacity to sin is possible. To choose to walk in the Holy Spirit each day and let Him be my life is to choose not to live in sin.

I remember things Annie liked, or what Daphne would say as I go through each day. They were woven into the fabric of my soul. I am not any one of them, but a multifaceted combination; one person with many enhancements.

The difference between life now and before is huge. The mental anguish for which I had no answers is gone. As are different people arguing with me–or with each other in my mind. Each holding their own story of abuse and torment is gone. They've been heard, healed, touched by God, loved, and validated. They've completed their season for being. I now have sweet peace with no more tortured memories.

Thank You, God, for being there for me. You are the center of my being.

Journal Entry

Father, I have many fears about an upcoming church trip and my declining physical health. Oh Jesus, take away the fear. I have strange feelings about it. Lord, I really don't want to tell anybody about the fears I've had unless You nudge me to.

Please let me have that quiet, gentle spirit You have been nurturing in me this past year. I want You to shine through me, Jesus. To be Your vessel, for You are the One who needs to be seen, not me.

You, my God, will hold me and lift me up through present challenges. You are my strength, my strong tower. You are the only One who can make sense of my life. Wherever we go from here, Lord, please hold tight to my hand. I don't want to try it on my own.

Praise you, Lord, for I am one. Thank you for bringing all of my people together. Today, I feel a little disconcerted about who I am. Dr. Kathy said when everyone integrated, personalities would remain only as enhancements. But where does that leave me as a whole?

I need You, Jesus. Learning to be a single personality–or rather adjusting to being an individual–is strange at times. It's like I've grown up now, but I'm surprised when I realize it. It's actually not all that hard behaving like an adult now, it's just different.

There was Annie then and so many other children before. When in a store, I notice things they would have liked to play with. I no longer act like a child and play with the toy or beg for ice cream.

I still enjoy children and miss leading Children's Choir but the yearning I had before to be with them is gone. Their love fulfilled my need for love and acceptance for who I was. I'm sure I needed to love them too.

"Dr. Kathy speaking."

"Hello, Dr. Kathy. This is Faith."

"Hello, Faith. How are you today?"

"Okay, I guess. I'm a little confused. It's a very different feeling being integrated these last six months. I've been remembering Annie and some of the others lately. Not in a bad way, but in a loving, fond way. Appreciating the fact that I'm no longer split into all those people, but now a whole person.

"I've been trying to write the book you and Viv suggested. I'm having difficulty finding a way to express how it feels to be one person."

"It's okay to grope in finding words. It's part of the process. Perhaps writing more poetry will help. That's where your gift truly flows."

"When I first integrated, I felt kind of numb. Like when all the alters went to the back and either I dissociated from myself or they buffered me. But then I began to realize no more conversations were going on inside my mind. Everything was so quiet–so peaceful. A little unnerving, too. I can't recall ever hearing one voice so I have no grid for what it's supposed to feel like. Am I supposed to feel this way? I feel as though the personalities were woven into the fabric of my soul. I'm not one of them, but a multifaceted combination. One person with many assets."

"Like many beautiful varied colored ribbons woven into one beautiful piece of fabric."

Yeah. That's beautiful.

"I think of Annie and smile to myself when I pass the toy section in a store. I think Annie would have liked this and would have wanted to play with this toy. Annie was special to me. Even though she brought up a lot of pain by revealing memories, I loved her so much. Now I love that part of me that is Annie. I miss Annie, but I rejoice in the fact that neither she nor I have the pain she carried."

"That's understandable. You have to mourn for them as you would the loss of any loved one."

"In the very beginning, I was tempted to bring people back. But after working so hard to integrate and the healing that came with it I knew even if I could, I wouldn't."

Journal Entry

I miss Maymee. I imagine she would look like Della Reese. She has a personality like her. I would like to sing like Maymee. Will I ever be able to? What would I sound like? Dare I know?

Dear Maymee,

Tried to write a poem to you. I can't get it going, so decided to write a letter instead.

Maymee, I miss you. You are the one person I depended upon the most. To protect me, to comfort me, to bring me laughter and a true expression of yourself. When I was with you I felt safe and loved. I'm sorry for what the mother did to you. I'm glad you made it through.

Now we are all integrated and I've lost you. Can't even find myself. I'd like to bring you back.

Remember the time we were on our way to group and you looked into the mirror and saw a white girl staring back at you? Almost had to pull over to the side of the road! Dr. Kathy said that was normal.

Or how about the MLK choir? You were the palest person there–with blond hair no less! I swear, Maymee, I wish I looked exactly like you now. You're so beautiful. There's no way I can change the color of my skin. God, that hurts.

I love you, Maymee, the memory of you, your voice, your smell, your lullabies over me.

Thank you, Maymee.
Thank you for being there.
Thank you for keeping me safe and for loving me.
Thanks for being you.
I love you, Maymee.
Goodbye, my dearest Maymee. Goodbye.
– Faith

Journal Entry

Thank you, Lord, for the meeting with Dan last night. He is so special to me. I discovered something interesting–I no longer need him. Daphne was very addicted to him and needed him way too much. He was a great instrument for her healing. Dan will always be special to me.

Journal Entry

I miss Maymee. Dr. Kathy says all my people who integrated are still a part of me. They are just not separate anymore. We talked about me visualizing what Maymee would say to me in different situations.

Maymee was my nurturing, strong mama. She sang to me and called me Baby Girl. She loved me a lot. She loved You a lot too, Jesus. It feels like she is gone forever.

I want to sing like Maymee. Dr. Kathy and I talked about Steve not liking black gospel music. Dr. Kathy thinks I could slowly grow into the style I want to sing.

We talked about the time Dad made fun of me to friends for singing in a black church. He then played my recording at the family reunion as though he was proud of me. He intended to bring glory to himself at my expense.

Journal Entry

I'm no longer split so now I have everybody's memories. This week has been unusually busy inside my mind. I've been remembering people and events that I haven't thought of for a long time. It almost feels like a manic episode. Dr. Kathy says it's because I'm remembering as a whole now instead of fragmented. It's all a little weird.

Went to group for multiple personalities last night with Dr. Kathy. It was great to see the girls again. It was a good session. I shared about being integrated. About struggling to find myself and coping without depending on the alters.

Journal Entry

Father, please help me discover who You created me to be. Lord, with the past people now integrated, I'm not sure what percentage of each person I am. Maybe I'm a totally new person. Emerging with lines no longer clearly drawn—blended together like a pastel sketch.

Whenever I'm disappointed at myself for being grouchy when dealing with chronic disease I wonder which of my alters was more gracious. Which alter passed the pain on? Who endured this disease as graciously as possible, showing God's power?

I was likely the hider, not the gracious endurer. I want to whine when pain comes. I hate it and don't want to deal with it. Then I hate myself for not handling it more positively.

I'm resisting having to learn to cope with life as a separate whole person. How much easier it was to let my people do it for me. Sometimes I wonder if I should have integrated it all.

On a positive note, I got a new walker. It's gorgeous, pretty green with a seat, basket, and handbrakes. It's great. I also got batteries for my scooter, so now I should be able to go places.

Journal Entry

I need You today, Father. I didn't handle yesterday very well at all. I don't think I even tried. I was frightened and angry when I began to spill and drop things and lose my balance. There was a time I would have loved the drama and attention this disease brings. Not now. I want to scream, "Take it away. No, no, no. I don't want to deal with it." But Life won't take back this hand she's dealt me. I haven't the power to destroy it and I don't have the option to fold.

1998

Journal Entry

More group and more private sessions with Dr. Kathy. Same old stuff. Good days, bad days. Emotional highs and lows. Putting out emotional fires of doubt, performance, acceptance. Etc., etc., etc. Calgon, take me away!

Is there ever an end to it all? Is there ever a place of healing–of walking with God–without therapists and therapy? I wonder.

Journal Entry

Depressed. I'm upset with Dr. Kathy for bringing yet another group member on board even though I expressed reluctance to add new people. I rebelled and just didn't show up–twice. I don't know–maybe I'm kind of tired of group. Feels like I've been in therapy for millions of years. Maybe a break would be good.

My people are integrated. I still struggle to cope as my whole put-together self-wishing many times I had some of them to lean on as in past times. What kind of person have I become? One who likes to be alone and quiet when not listening to music way too loud.

Who am I? A child of God, in whom He loves and delights. He waits for me to talk to Him each day and remember to commune with Him. When I feel blah He's still there, knowing how I feel, but wanting me to "tell Him all about it." He wants to share the yucky days, too. His love is big enough for it all. I've felt so out of touch with Him and allowed shame to drag me further down. He knew where I was emotionally and where I'll be tomorrow.

You are my God, Jesus. I don't deserve Your love. Nor do I deserve Your salvation. You are my strength, my all in all. If only I could tell You in a new way with fresh words how much You mean to me, Lord. I love you, Jesus. I guess I don't need to feel goosebumps when I tell You I love You, huh? That's what has been bothering me lately. I don't feel the emotions I think I should be feeling. Maybe that's due to medication or hormones. Who knows, Lord? Oh, You do.

I don't want to lose You, Jesus–not as in losing my salvation–but as in losing my daily relationship with You. That's what it's felt like lately.

Oh, Jesus, You are my peace.
You are my comfort.
You are my anchor, my rock, my love, my confidante.
Oh, Jesus, please draw me to Your side when I'm too full of myself.
Let me focus more on You than on myself.

1999

Journal Entry

Justified, I am justified through Christ. God sees me as justified.

I wander around in a quandary about what others think of me. Why? I need acceptance, love, and understanding. Or do I? If God already loves, accepts, and understands me, why must I struggle to win the battle of acceptance? The war of love and understanding?

It's a choice–or so they say. "Quit obsessing about trying to please your Abba Daddy. Stop it and trust God who is your Good Father." Okay, I hear ya, but that's not an easy thing to do. These men who are in authority over me remind me of my daddy in some ways. It makes me want to scream, "You're too rigid! I can't breathe!"

Memories. I can't keep them from coming into my mind. I don't think I'm obsessing about them. Only You know for sure.

Spirituality. Father, am I spiritual? If I'm in You, then I'm spiritual. Sometimes I don't feel like I'm in You. I feel like I'm someone who is not in tune with You. One who doesn't know You like I should. It doesn't make sense, I know. But it's reality for me for now, anyway.

Have I begun to use dissociation again in order to handle things? Yes, on some days, I have. Maybe that's when I don't feel connected to You, Lord. Help me, Lord! I'm screaming inside. Help me!

You guide me, my Lord. I know beyond a shadow of a doubt if I listen and obey. You alone, Lord, I give it to You. May have to give it to You many times, but I know You love me. You'll take the load when I can't stand. Cause me to walk in Your strength when You know I can—even if I think I can't.

You are faithful in Your love. You are faithful in Your discipline. Please teach me about this aspect of Your love. Love disciplines. You are never unfair, Lord. Sometimes people are. Please hold me through the hardship, the anger, and despair. Please guide me to handle it Your way, and not my own.

Make me mature in You. Let my confidence grow in You. As my faith increases, so let my wonder of You. And the joy of knowing You. Overcome my thoughts to triumph in victory in Your strength.

Howard

♪ Because You Love Me ♪

If I dwell in the shelter of the Most High
I will say He is my fortress.
If I dwell in the shadow of His wings
I will say He is my guide.
As He covers me with His faithfulness
I will hear Him say to me
Because you love Me
I will come close to you
To protect and lift you up.
When you call upon Me
I will answer.
I'll be with you
Because you love Me.

Your hands made me and fashioned me;
Give me understanding,
so that I may learn Your commandments.
May those who fear You see me and be glad,
Because I wait for Your word.
I know, O LORD, that Your judgments are righteous,
And that You have afflicted me in faithfulness.
May Your favor comfort me,
According to Your word to Your servant.
May Your compassion come to me that I may live,
For Your law is my delight.

Psalm 119:73-77 (NASB)

2000

"Hi, Viv. How's the family?"

"We're doing okay. I'm sorry I haven't been in touch lately."

"I understand. I know you're busy with five children."

"You got that right! Laundry is a full-time job. But now that the youngest is no longer a baby I'm starting to fall into a semi-productive routine."

"I can't even imagine!" Smiling. "I'm going to start seeing a prayer counselor at church next week. His name is Howard. He's a very sweet and gentle man."

"I'm glad you're getting prayer counseling. Psychiatry without the Holy Spirit leading the session seems to be just spinning your wheels."

"I'm finding I still have a lot of Steve issues to work through. It's painful but not agonizing like it was before. Now that I no longer have alters to deal with each situation, I'm having to learn how to cope on my own. I've also had to grieve their absence."

"Makes sense to me."

"I think I'm going to like Howard. He's a pulls-no-punches-goes straight-to-the-heart-of-the-matter kind of guy."

"That's great. Sounds like you're well on your way."

"Maybe, but it sure has taken a long time. I expected all my troubles to be over once I integrated. It took a long time to get used to it."

"Probably because you kept regurgitating everything in group sessions instead of letting the Holy Spirit direct your therapy."

"You're probably right."

"I'm very excited for you."

"Me, too."

"Hi, Howard. I'm Faith Alison."

"Hello, Faith. Please come in and take a seat."

"Thank you."

"Tell me about yourself and what your goals are for prayer counseling."

"Well, I have a chronic disease. I'm having to change my lifestyle to accommodate my declining health. I used to do many tasks at one time, but now I'm having to exert more effort just to get one thing accomplished."

"Do you have performance issues?"

"Yes. I don't know why, but I still do. You see, I lived with Multiple Personality Disorder due to child abuse from both parents. I was healed in February 1997. I dealt with performance issues then, but I think my health may have brought it all up again because I can't function as I used to."

"Many people who are more debilitated than you lead productive lives. Someone who has been abused as you often experiences isolation, loneliness, feeling like they don't fit in…"

"I'm experiencing those issues in dealing with my illness."

"You keep skirting around the issue."

The pen I'm tapping on my leg breaks with a sharp SNAP. "On everything?"

"No, just on performance issues. It would be natural for an abuse victim such as yourself to be dependent on others, such as a counselor. One-on-one interaction satisfies your needs."

"Does that mean I shouldn't be in counseling?"

"No. It is probably because of the abuse that you might easily become dependent." Discussion continues until time to end the session. We close with a prayer.

"You were very generic in your goals I asked about. I want you to think of specific goals you want to accomplish with counseling. Take time to think about whether or not you want to continue in counseling with me."

"Oh, I do."

Smiling. "Next session I'll give you a pencil."

Divorcing Dr. Kathy for our entire family to seek prayer counseling with Howard could prove to be interesting.

Howard starts sessions with prayer.

"Father in heaven, thank You for this time that I can come to pray with Howard. We invite You, Holy Spirit, to direct this time. Reveal what we need to pray about. What issues we need to work on and what to give to You.

"Howard, I don't know why, but I keep shifting from knowing God intellectually to relying on Him."

"Finding a place of dependency on God, stepping out in faith in the specific aspect of His character requires trust. You have to risk trusting God to be something that until up to this point you didn't trust Him in."

"Like trusting Him to take care of my family."

"Exactly, if you haven't trusted Him in that area before."

"I don't know why I keep losing faith. He's always been there for us, but when things look grim I get anxious over and over again. I guess I keep thinking God expects us to take care of ourselves. Through responsibility–or as adults or something. Like maybe He doesn't want to be bothered with every little detail and says, 'Why don't you grow up?'"

"Your earthly father's influence has given you a misperception of a father that's in the way of seeing God. I want you to list as many different character traits of your dad as you can for our next session, okay?"

"Okay."

"Let's pray...

Most of the two-hour session is spent in prayer with Scripture verses highlighted throughout. What a refreshing difference!

Journal Entry

Spent most of the day in bed not feeling well. Started on new pain meds last night for chronic disease. I think it makes me sleepy during the day.

Thank You, Lord, for yet another Monday, another beginning. I love You, Lord. You are my all in all. I don't feel so spiritual today, Lord. It's probably mostly physical. Please forgive me, my Lord, I need to be in Your word more and more consistent with my writing.

Thanks for the song idea You gave me last week. Please help me fine-tune it, Father. Thanks for the car You provided! Thank You for the people in our lives You put here to advise us. Please forgive me for wanting our old car back. How I did enjoy it. Change is difficult for me. Please walk with me today. I love You, Lord.

Journal Entry

Today I think I'm feeling less drugged by painkillers. Backed the dosage down to one instead of two. Still feel on edge, nervous. I feel kind of blah today.

Thanks for this quiet time, though, Lord. I like having alone, quiet time with You.

Feeling symptoms of the disease–fatigue, etc. Will I ever feel normal again? What is normal? Have I accepted the fact that I'm still going to have this disease regardless of who or what I am?

I am me. I am not a disease. I am a person with dreams, hopes, likes and dislikes. Disease does not define me.

Disease is something I have to cope with regularly, like bad breath, mud, and rotten fish. No, those are things I can do something about. I can brush my teeth, chew gum, step around the mud, and throw rank fish out. Disease is not something I can refuse. When I ignore pain in my body, it screams louder and louder until I finally listen and acknowledge the truth. What can I say?

Thank You, Lord. Today I can:

- walk
- move
- read
- take a bath
- breathe
- meditate and think
- write

I've started a Bible study and discussion in my home for people with chronic illnesses. During tonight's meeting, I shared with the group thoughts I had from Scripture verses.

"Look what I found in Psalms 119 'It is good for me that I was afflicted, So that I may learn Your statutes.' I think God afflicted me to draw me closer to Him."

"I don't believe God would afflict His children except in chastisement." A participant, Tom, contradicts this.

"Through God's Word, He turned my focus from me and my disease to Him and the fact that He is the One in control."

"That's good, but 'by His stripes we are healed'' and 'He took up our infirmities.' He heals all our diseases. He took care of our sins and our diseases on the cross."

"So Tom, why aren't we healed? Why are you still suffering from asthma?"

"It's my own fault I'm not healed. I must not be walking out my faith. We are to stand on faith–unwavering."

I'm so confused by all Tom said about healing and faith. It shakes my foundation, all I've been standing on–the lifeline I believed God had given me to stand on.

Group members are gone. The pain of doubt and confusion manifests itself in uncontrollable weeping. Wish I were stronger. I need someone to validate what God had told me.

Steve and Josh discover me crying.

"Tom was only trying to help, Mama, but that was only his opinion."

"A lot of people feel the way Tom does."

"Mama, if God gave you a verse then stand on it."

I'm thankful for their love and concern. We're behaving like a real family. Still depressed, but at least the crying has stopped.

"Something in Psalm 119 jumped out at me this week, Howard. Verse 75 says, 'You have afflicted me in faithfulness' and verse 67 'Before I was afflicted I went astray, but now I obey Your commands.' I've been trying to tell God what He was going to do–demanding that He heal me–all in faith, mind you."

"What changed? Your focus on the disease and yourself or God?"

"The fact that He is the One in control. During my Chronic Disease Bible study group, I shared what God's been telling me in Psalm 119. One of the participants said he doesn't believe God would afflict His children except in chastisement. It made me start to question my interpretation."

"I believe your conviction from God's Word is correct."

"I wish I were stronger."

"You're beating yourself up. Be at peace."

"That's what I'm praying for."

"Good."

Journal Entry

Hello, Lord. I want to know You more. Please let me have a Mt. Sinai experience. I want to draw close to You like Moses did when You came down to draw Your children to know You. Please let me not run or stand "afar off" as they did for fear of Your power.

Father, in discovering my sinful self, I think it is impossible for me in my strength to live a day without sinning. How can this be? Please give me enough of Your power to leave my old self behind and live in Your power–in the power of the Holy Spirit.

Do what You will with me for Your glory. Nothing I've done, Lord, causes me to deserve Your power. But Your Son, Jesus Christ paid the ultimate price for my sins when He died on the cross. So, I am covered with His blood. Only through Him can I be worthy to come into Your manifest presence.

Father, if that's what You want, I desire it. Do You want Your children to seek You in this manner? Please show me by Your Spirit. Speak to my heart. Your Word tells me to seek Your face. I love Your face, my King. I love You, Lord. Please fill me so overabundantly that others will be touched in whatever way You want to touch them, Lord. Your will be done.

2000

I recently listened to a sermon on humility. As a child of God, our main character trait should automatically be humility. Humility was defined as not thinking less of ourselves, but thinking less *about* ourselves. Getting our minds off ourselves and onto what God wants us to do and think about. I need to think less about me and my affairs but not less of my worth, because I am a child of the King, bought with a price, Jesus' blood.

I am glad the preacher clarified the definition because it's something that's always confused me. Working in therapy for so long caused me to think more highly of myself while knowing I'm a sinner saved by grace. The two never really seemed to jive, yet in my depression, the issue of self had to be addressed. Maybe I'm confused because I kept focusing on my self-esteem (my regard) instead of my self-worth. My value as a human being and a child of God. Now, my Lord is my self-worth.

Had a headache–seems like all night–then woke up with one this morning. Tomorrow I have a session with Howard. Makes me anxious just thinking about it. My stomach knots up a little.

Am I making any progress? Will we have to backtrack on every single tiny thing? Should I have switched to Howard? I feel disloyal to Dr. Kathy. Need to write her a letter to thank her for all the help she's given. Must write to the DID group, also.

Oh, Father, I need You to lead me along. Please forgive me when I feel "zoned out." Please forgive my sins. Thank You for Your love.

Cry Out to God

Goodbye to Me

Lord, I want to be a servant of the King.
And I want my life inspired by all He brings
But for this, I must die.
Sometimes it's hard to understand the reasons why.
Is there a way I can save a piece of me?
Isn't there some way You could take this cup from me?
I hear You whispering, "This is how it must be."
But my God it's awfully hard to say goodbye to me.

Hold me close as I say goodbye to me.
My heart knows You're all I need.
I'll stay right here on my knees until I find the strength
To say goodbye to me.
Because I'm tired of living somewhere in between
My love for You and my love for me.
Take whatever is left of me, I sacrifice it, Lord, to Thee.
Goodbye to me.

> Answer me when I call,
> God of my righteousness!
> You have relieved me in my distress;
> Be gracious to me and hear my prayer.
> But know that the LORD has set apart
> the godly person for Himself;
> the LORD hears when I call to Him.
> Tremble, and do not sin;
> Meditate in your heart upon your bed,
> and be still.
>
> Psalm 4:1,3,4 (NASB)

2000

"Have you any specific goals for us to work on?" Howard asks.

"I don't feel as close to God as I have before. When I was in prayer sessions for DID, God built a safe house for Daphne and wooed her. I need that for me."

"That was you. You were fragmented, true, but believing those fragmentations were other people is believing a falsehood. Even if what happened to you was horrific, that's not what's important right now. What you *believe* as a result is what's important. Your reality needed to be processed and handled correctly with truth. It still does. Daphne was imaginary, so all that was done for her was actually done for you. You are the one He wants to dance with, the one He wrote His song for."

"But I need Jesus to do the same for *me* as He did for Daphne."

"Isn't Daphne you?"

"Yes."

"Well then, what keeps you from accepting the fact that what He did for her He did for you, since she is you?"

"Logically I accept it, but I don't *feel* like I, *Faith*, experienced it."

"Why can't you accept the fact that God did build a safe house for *you*? I agree that you fragmented and compartmentalized the fragments. When you decided to give a name to each of these fragments, that's when you gave them individual personalities. They were very real to you, yes–but now they are integrated. All the things God did for them were all for you since they were all a part of you. What keeps you from accepting the fact that God did all these things for you?"

"Well, logically–I do believe He has."

"Then what?"

"It just doesn't *feel* like I've experienced it. Maybe I should read my journal and replace Daphne's name with mine."

"That sounds like a great idea. Erase all their names and put yours in their place. Then read it. Do you need more assurance of God's love?"

"Yes!"

"Do you think you will ever be to the point where you won't need the reassurance of His love?"

"No."

"Okay then, since you will always need the reassurance of His love–how will you be shown that love?"

"By His Word and power or the Holy Spirit."

"That's right. Let's pray and give all your good attributes to God."

"Father, I give all the good things about me to you. My creativity, musical abilities–everything–I give to You. I give You my childlike faith, my strength, my ability to relate to various types of people, my passion for lost souls, my sense of humor–I give it all to You."

"Father, let Faith be filled to overflowing with joy and Your love…"

Howard and I talk through my dreams. "A common thread of being a powerless victim is normal because of how your life has been. Let me know if you have any dreams where you're climbing. Visions you had of climbing up on Jesus' lap are good."

"I had a dream the other night. Steve and I were living in a house with big windows with no curtains. I'm fearful of danger, exposure–being alone. The wood on the porch outside is weathered and gray.

"I then went to visit my friend Vivien. They had a large house. I wanted a nap so I went to their daughters' room. The bed was covered with folded laundry. I moved the clothes and started to lie down, but the daughters came home and wanted their room. I went searching for another bed–no empty room. I thought, 'The Lord sure has blessed them with all this space.'"

"Have you ever had a room of your own?"

"No. I've never had anything that was just mine."

"Let's pray the Lord will give you a room all your own."

Jesus built a safe house for Daphne. Wasn't that also for me? Am I integrated or not?

"Howard, reading Daphne's story is bringing up sexual abuse at a deeper level. It's more detailed than before. It makes me sick to my stomach."

"You must be stronger now. That's a good thing."

"What do you mean?"

"God has revealed memories to you in increments that you can handle. He started gradually and as you've dealt with each He's able to show you more intense memories to deal with. He let you strengthen your faith and resolve to fight the battle. You can look back to see how He's been with you so you don't have to fear what's ahead."

"Daddy was so good, so fun in the daytime and so bad at night. He was like two different people."

"What's our overall picture of him? All dark or all light?"

"A mixture of both."

"How do you think God sees the overall scene?"

"He was watching. He did not like it."

"How did He see your dad?"

"He was doing wrong."

"What did God do?"

"God told him to stop."

"How did God see you?"

"He saw what was happening to me and saw me in pain."

"What did He do?"

"He was crying with me. He was grieving with me."

"Why would God tell your dad to stop?"

"Because He is a fair righteous God. Because God is sovereign. Because what my dad was doing was wrong. He wanted Daddy to repent. He wanted me to be treated with natural love the way He intended. It's ugly." I scowled. "This sort of thing usually is, right?"

Journal Entry

Sexual abuse. Deeper levels. Why must I look at it in such great detail, Father? It brings up strong feelings of denial, of disbelief, of not wanting to admit any of it. Not my daddy.

Maybe it's all in my imagination. Maybe I've heard too many other horror stories. Been too influenced by my friends sharing what happened to them. Read too many accounts of sexual abuse. Maybe in some sick way, I just want to get attention, even if it's only from one person, a doctor, or a counselor. Am I really that wacko?

WRETCHED ANGUISH! ABSOLUTE REVULSION! Current flashback of my daddy-more sexual abuse, even more disgusting than before. It's so vivid-so horrid-it sneaks up and backhands me in the face! My head spins. I'm taken completely off guard.

It hurts, Jesus. It *hurts*! I don't want to cry anymore. I'm so very tired. Lord, if I can't escape, what can I do? Lord, show me what to do.

Please let Howard return my call. Oh, Father, I need help. It's hard not to escape. I just want to run away. If I only knew where to run to. I just might do it-if I had a plan and somewhere or someone to go to. But that wouldn't be a very nice thing to do to Steve and Josh. They haven't done anything to deserve me abandoning them. Guess that was a bad idea. What else can I do except escape somewhere in my psyche?

I must DO SOMETHING! I can't remain in this emotional torment any longer. I feel myself shutting down right now, not allowing the tears to flow. It's been half an hour and Howard hasn't called. He's probably involved in something, a session maybe, preventing him from returning my call. In desperation, I call a friend I know from the DID group I used to attend.

"Hello, Samantha? This is Faith. Can you talk for a while?"

"Sure, you sound upset. What's the matter?"

I'm crying now. "Oh, Sam. I had an awful flashback and can't get a hold of my counselor. I desperately need someone to talk to. Can I share it with you?"

"Yes."

"Thank you. It was so awful I can't share it with just anyone, but I just have to tell someone! If I keep it in any longer I'll explode. I just don't know how to handle it. It makes me feel like I'm splitting into a child again."

"Why don't you let the little girl tell me about it?" So sweet. So understanding. So obliging.

"I remember something nasty my daddy made me do. It makes me gag just to think of it." I share vivid details of the memory with her.

"Oh, Faith. That's awful. It makes me so angry that he did that to you. You're too young for me to tell you what I'd like to do to him! Faith, why don't you let the river from the throne of God wash you clean of this memory?"

"Okay."

"Do you like to play?"

"Uh-huh. I have some shiny copper pennies I like to play with."

"Why don't you come out and play with your pennies or color–whatever you like to do for a while each day?"

"I don't know about that, Sam." Wisdom intervenes. "I truly want to be grown up about this and stay in reality."

"Then let the little girl come out and talk to be able to process what has happened to her. She can call and talk to me anytime."

"We'll see."

"Howard, I'm so glad you returned my call. I've had a recent flashback about my daddy that was so vivid and so hideous I can't even talk about it. I called a friend and talked with her and I've been pouring it out to God in my journal all day. It makes me want to split just to escape the memory!"

"You must stop writing and start speaking out loud to God. Are you alone?"

"Yes."

"You don't need me or a friend. You need to talk to God. Allow your feelings to flow. Hold nothing back. Abandon yourself to the Lord, not in writing because thoughts are faster than your hand can write. Direct all the corruption uncensored to God. When you do this it invites God to show up."

"I've been writing all day."

"No. Cry out to God in total abandon. Vomit all the junk out to God, having an uncensored exchange with God until you are totally spent."

"I *am* totally spent."

"You must *fight it out* with God, Faith. I don't know what is causing you to want to dissociate or whatever, but I know God is your answer. Not your friend, not me, but *God!*"

"Okay. I only called you for guidance, Howard. Thank you."

Howard chuckles. "You don't sound very thankful."

Cocooning myself in an afghan, I cry out loud to God. "Lord, I feel so alone. I really hate flashbacks! How could a man like my daddy be such a monster? You know what he did to me, Lord...It was awful. I wanted to throw up! I want to throw up now just remembering it!

"I hate him! I want to dig up his body and desecrate it by exposing his remains. I want to write in the sky what he did to me so everyone would know the truth about him. I hate my mom and my brother for either not realizing what was happening or for not stopping him.

"Oh Lord, suddenly I see myself as a little girl running to Daddy's lap. How very much I loved him and wanted to please him. And then he treated me that way! I suppose I could have resisted or refused, so in this case, I cooperated. That's so confusing to me because I really didn't want to do it. I figured I'd die if I didn't or I'd probably die if I did. Either way felt as though I would die.

"I don't want to give up dissociating," I blubber. "I don't want to give up the child who likes shiny pennies."

"I don't know what to do with this. Only You know. I need You, Lord, to tell me what to do. How do I handle this? I need You to hold me, Lord."

I sense His presence. He enfolds me in His love.

I know how very tired you are. Let Me love the little girl in you. I like shiny things too. That is why I created copper and other pretty metals. I love and accept you just as you are. I accept you where you are emotionally and spiritually today without condemnation. I don't condemn you for feeling like a child or the need to be childish.

"Forgive me for hating my family."

I forgive you.

Asleep in His arms I don't even need the doll for comfort. Jesus is my Comforter. I feel like I've been run over by a train, completely exhausted. I'm sad, but I have a deep sense of peace because He loves and accepts me. It's so incredible.

This is only the beginning–learning to abandon myself to You, Lord. Knowing You are the Only One who matters in my recovery. You, Jesus, hold the keys to my heart, soul, and mind, to my total healing. Thank You for Who You are to me.

Gratitude brings a measure of joy. Thanking and praising You brings joy. I'm tired, but no longer am I devastated by this demon from my past. It's gone, erased, forgotten, dealt with, and forgiven once more. Forgiven.

Journal Entry

New flashbacks, more pain, and anger have surfaced again. I'm just a puddle of pain in God's hands. Why? I forgave my father years ago. Must I do it again?

Howard says that to be rid of the pain, to break the tie from the past, the key is forgiveness. Forgiveness is the key to release me from *anger*, not *pain*.

But haven't I already forgiven my parents? Is it an everyday thing? I have to incorporate it into my life on a daily, sometimes hourly basis. If so, will there come a time when I will think of the abuse and no longer feel the pain and no longer have the need to forgive?

If my father were here with all pretense aside perhaps he would beg my forgiveness for all the times he touched me. Maybe he would. Maybe he wouldn't. God would be the one to forgive him. Then perhaps I would choose to forgive, but it would just be lip service, not from the heart. If God were to forgive me that way I don't think I'd be totally forgiven.

He said, "As you forgive others, so I will forgive you." So in that case I'm up the proverbial creek. On the other hand, God promises to make us His children when we accept His Son and repent of our sins.

As someone once said, "God doesn't expect forgiveness to be easy. If it were, we'd do it willingly. He wouldn't have to ask."

Feeling childish and very needy this morning. I brought the baby doll Vivien gave me to my session with Howard.

"Look, Howard. My dog chewed the hands and toes of my baby doll. Can you fix her?" I try to give the doll to him.

"I can't fix it. That's not what I do."

I hug her and cry.

"What is it you want to do today?"

"Play."

"I will not allow you to escape reality. I'm not here to play. What do you like to do when you play?"

"Something with my doll," I mutter through tears.

"Sit up straight so you can look me in the eyes," Howard commanded. "I'm not here to fix your doll. I'm not here to play. This is not a doll hospital. I'm here to help you."

"I want you to fix the broken child inside me," I murmur.

"Put the doll down, Faith." I cry and squeeze her tighter. "You're using the doll for comfort instead of allowing Jesus to be your comfort. That's idolatry."

"The doll's not an idol. How is it idolatry?"

"It's idolatry when you replace Jesus with the doll."

I set the doll on the floor. I then lay face down on the floor to pray, a symbol of total surrender. Howard prays aloud with me.

"Jesus, please help me seek You. Thank You Holy Spirit for showing me my selfishness. Please forgive me. Jesus, I don't like new memories of abuse. It hurts so much, but I ask You to continue to help me remember so I can be completely free."

After much prayer, Howard says, "Dissociation is self-deception to your detriment. Dissociation is a figment of your imagination using the power of creativity to avoid reality. That is a misuse of the application of God's gift."

"It was a matter of survival!"

"'For whoever wants to save their life will lose it, but whoever loses their life for me will find it.' His acceptance of sinners is based on repentance. Self-deception is a sinful practice. Dissociation with knowledge is a sin. You must first see it for what it is, rather than deny it."

"I admit self-deception is a sin. Father, I realize dissociation is a sin because it is relying on my ability to escape rather than trusting You to heal. Please forgive me for attempting to run from the memories."

"Don't beat yourself up over this, Faith. We all deceive ourselves at times through denial, suppression, or dissociation." Bless Howard. "Father, please bring new ways for Faith to express her creativity without the practice of self-deception."

"That reminds me of new songs God has recently given me. He has already given that creative outlet as an answer! Wow! Now I can wait and watch to see what God has planned for me with anticipation!"

"Since you created a new persona, you obviously haven't truly dealt with the memory."

"So what do I do now?"

"Pray. Ask for God's presence. In light of His presence–whatever oppresses you has to fall off. Ask Him to wash away any defilement. Ask Him to walk through the flashback or any memory with you. Embrace the pain that comes and let the Holy Spirit comfort you."

"Holy Spirit, fill us and lead this session." Waiting on the Lord. "Howard, I need to tell you exactly what Daddy did and share a new memory with you…" I tell him through a deluge of tears.

"Father, grant Faith comfort from Your Holy Spirit."

Sobbing begins to diminish. "I just feel so much shame."

"You don't have to be ashamed. What was done to you was wrong, but it was not your shame. The only way to lay down your father's shame is to forgive him. Jesus forgave each of us when He bore our sins on the cross. He also bore the sins of your father and forgave him, too."

"Yes, but I don't think Daddy will be in heaven."

"Perhaps not."

"I wonder why I didn't become promiscuous like some abuse victims?"

"I believe you had a sense of right and wrong."

"Well, Daddy didn't teach it to me–that's for sure."

"Victims who are promiscuous usually do so out of rebellion and anger. They also long for acceptance and attention, seeking for it in sexual relationships."

"Now that I'm aware of what I've been doing, I realize I sure can dissociate easily, can't I?"

"You need to face things head-on, like we're doing today."

2001

"Hello, Howard. This is Faith. I've been very depressed over the weekend. I've been having thoughts of suicide. Would you please talk to me?"

"Have you done anything, taken pills, or cut yourself?"

"No."

"What's Steve's work number? I'll try to get a hold of him. Would you call a Mental Hospital Crisis hotline?"

"No."

"I have a meeting to attend. I can call you this afternoon. Will you call a friend to stay with you until I can get through to Steve?"

"Okay."

"Hello, Marilyn. This is Faith. Howard asked me to call you because I've been feeling suicidal lately..." Several minutes later. "Hold on a minute. Someone is knocking at the door." Returning to the phone, "Oh man, I'm so humiliated! I have to let you go, the police are at my door!"

"Look you guys, I'm fine. *Really, I'm fine!*" The two men in blue don't look convinced.

"It's okay, officers." Steve is coming up the sidewalk. "I'll take care of her."

"Steve! I guess Howard called you."

"Yes."

"Are you her husband?"

"Yes, sir."

"Are you going to take her to a hospital, or shall we?"

"I will."

I'm lying in a community hospital psych unit wondering why I'm here. I was very depressed over the weekend. I called Howard for some help and here I am. Upsetting. I called him again to tell him the hospital won't allow him to come for a session today. He said it was okay. It's *not* okay! I'm livid. He tells me God has a reason for it all. He will make all things work for the good. I wonder.

I've been on an emotional roller coaster today. Woke in physical pain between four and six a.m. Pain meds helped enough to get a little more sleep.

"I'm in pain. I need something stronger than Tylenol," I tell a doctor.

"I'm here for the psyche. That's all I can help you with." No compassion.

"Are you feeling any better?"

"Yes."

"Do you want to go home?"

"No. I don't feel safe enough to go home yet."

"What about your family? Surely they'll be there for you."

"I don't think so. I want to stay."

"You've been here two and a half weeks. Insurance has approved a Day Hospital for You. You'll start on Monday."

PANIC! Need to call Howard! He's not returning my call! Where is he? My body is wracked with pain. My mood is in a spiral nosedive. I'd rather be dead than endure this pain. I try to dig at my arm searching for a vein.

"You need to go to group this evening," a nurse tells me.

"I'm in pain. I need to rest."

A second nurse enters the room. "If you're still feeling suicidal we may need to escort you to the quiet room."

"No, I'm okay."

"If you promise you'll call if you need assistance we won't take you away. I need you to promise you won't hurt yourself." Nurse One is sympathetic.

"I will."

"You're just angry with the doctor." Nurse Two–not so sympathetic.

"I realize I have no control over punishing the doctor or getting back at him. He had no compassion towards me or my pain caused by chronic disease. The Disabilities Act probably could kick his butt."

"You're acting childish. We need to reduce your privileges to level one since you refuse to go home."

"I'm not only dealing with depression but also chronic disease."

"I'm sorry you're hurting, but our main concern is for your safety."

"We don't have the facilities to keep you any longer. If you're not able to go home, you will need to commit yourself to the state hospital."

OH NO! Not there!

Shower spray washes away a downpour of tears. Once dressed, I sit on my bed, my back to the camera, completely disregarding the fact that I'm still on suicide watch. Using inconspicuous movements, I carefully open a king-sized Snickers bar. Not bothering to savor it, I stuff my mouth and chew.

A nurse bursts through the door. "What are you hiding? Let me see."

I hunker with my back to her and stuff the last piece into my mouth. Flinging the wrapper at her I shout, "Ith jutht a piethe o' candy, for cwyin' ou' wowd!"

God! Where are You? You promised to never leave or forsake me. Where are You when I need You? I can't do this anymore. It's completely out of my hands. I surrender every ounce of control. I abandon myself completely to Your will. I place my trust in You to protect me when I return home. My life is completely in Your hands.

Test results reveal a genetic hormonal imbalance requiring long-term antidepressants. I'm discharged and resume meeting with Howard.

PhD-Perfectly Healed & Delivered

Free

Free to be cut loose for eternity
My mask a mere shell cracked apart
Alone at last–no longer the distant past
With its dirty fingernails bloody as hell.

Love so pure I know for sure
All my shattered parts are healed by God.
Beginning anew at last it all rings true
No more voices inside taking control.

This is my final farewell.
I'm on a different path.
My spirit is free at last.

When I was a child,
I talked like a child, I thought like a child,
I reasoned like a child.
When I became a man,
I put the ways of childhood behind me.

For now, we see only a reflection as in a mirror;
then we shall see face to face.
Now I know in part;
then I shall know fully,
even as I am fully known.

And these three remain,
faith, hope, and love.
But the greatest of these is love.

1 Corinthians 13:11-13 (NASB)

2001

"How does all the work the Lord is doing in you affect your relationship with others?" Howard asks.

"I have more compassion for Steve than I used to."

"Do you consider yourself a treasure?"

"No. I feel like Steve got the short end of the stick."

"Why is that?"

"Steve has a larger capacity to love than I do. He loves me much more than I love him. I don't deserve him."

"Tell me about your love for God."

"Oh, I love Him. I need Him."

"Are you worthy of His love?"

"No," I reply feeling discouraged and depressed. My shoulders slump as I place my hands between my knees.

"I've worked with you and prayed with you for a year and I've been rather gentle with you, Faith, but this time I'm going for it. It's time for you to pry yourself out of the *getting* mindset of demanding your needs to be met and start gauging all of life as to what God wants for you. You need to renounce your childish desire to control everything in life, your friends, your family, and God.

"It takes faith to release pride, to move out in your natural daily expression of who you are in Christ. It takes faith to accept God's love for you. Stop viewing yourself as a victim and acknowledge who you are in Christ. You've been sitting there like a whimpering pup the entire time I've been talking to you. Look me in the eye, Faith. You are precious to God."

"Oh, Howard!" I grab tissues to dry my flooding eyes.

"Look at all the emotions this brings up. You are precious to God. You are a priceless treasure. Look me in the eyes, Faith. God loves you." Scooting his chair closer to mine, his face uncomfortably close. "Look me in the eyes. No, *look me in the eyes, Faith.* God loves *you.* You are beautiful in God's eyes."

Sobbing. "Yeah, right."

"Rejecting appreciation and approval wounds the one giving it. Rejecting God's love and identity as His beloved child wounds God. You are a blessing. You are perfect in Christ."

"I'm not perfect."

"Not on your merit, but when God looks at Faith, He sees Christ, who is perfect. God judges the heart. You are clothed in a robe of righteousness. There is no condemnation in Christ Jesus. You need to divorce yourself from the old identity and affirm your new identity, Christ.

"Move out of the victim mindset and see yourself for what you are now. Instead of beating yourself up when you get flashbacks or when you experience failure, you need to confess it and abandon yourself to God. Cry out to Him—verbalizing—with deep heartfelt prayer and *labor* until release or comfort comes. When Christ lives in you, a beautiful fragrance is released. He increases as you decrease. God restores a complete foundation of faith to walk in. Let's pray."

"Hi, Faith. What have you brought for us to work on today?"

"Well, Howard, I've come to accept the fact that Satan deceived me into believing the lie that I was incompetent and not able to be responsible. I've needed to let go of Daphne and Annie—to step out in faith that what I know in my mind is true and to stand on that truth in a spiritual battle with Satan. Satan doesn't want to give up the ground he has stolen from me. It's been a deception. An illusion that became my reality—that God did certain things for me as different personalities instead of God's truth that anything He did for any of the fragments of myself He did for *me* because *they were all me.*"

"You've got it."

"I still seem to have resistance to work on fear of emotional pain."

"You've faced that before. It's nothing new."

"Right."

"Incompetence, feeling like you'll never achieve wholeness or any form of success is a generational lie from your mother. You must come against that lie."

"You're right. I come against the lie of incompetence in the name of Jesus and break that and any generational curse.

"I've learned that forgiveness is not the key to healing damaged emotions."

"It's not?"

"No. Forgiveness is the key to deliverance from anger. The key to healing damaged emotions is God's love."

"I see...Tell me, Faith-from the depths of your heart-who are you?"

"Because of Christ, I am a forgiven child of God. I am a strong survivor and a victorious conqueror."

"Praise God! Faith Alison, I pronounce you graduated head of the class. You've earned your Ph.D.–Perfectly healed & Delivered in Christ. Now go minister to others."

2001

"Hello, Faith? My name is Terri. I go to Bethesda Church and heard about your Bible study for people with chronic diseases. I'd like to know if you still have an opening."

"Sure, come on. We meet from eleven to one, so bring a sack lunch."

"Your voice sounds familiar. Are you in the choir?"

"Yes."

"Did you recently have the elders pray over you?"

"Yes. I was asking for blessings on this Bible study."

"I'm in the choir, too. I was hoping that was you! I'm not really sure if this Bible study will do me much good."

"Oh?"

"I feel I should warn you, I have more problems than chronic disease. I'm also seeing a counselor at church for emotional pain. He's the one who recommended I attend your study."

"That won't be a problem. We'd love for you to join us."

"But you don't know my story."

"Well, you don't know *my* story."

"What's *your* story?"

"I was in psychiatric therapy for twenty years and four years ago God healed me of Multiple Personality Disorder."

GASP! "You won't believe this, but I have MPD! I've never been able to tell anyone else except my ex-husband and my therapist."

"It's no coincidence God has brought us together."

Hold on to your hat, Sister! Has God got a surprise in store for you!

Afterword

Faith Alison:

Howard once said even if a person's story seems too horrific to believe, that's not what's important. What the individual *believes* happened is what's important. Their reality is what needs to be processed and handled correctly.

Although my name has been changed and minor details have been included to fill the gaps of undocumented events, my testimony is true.

Remembering abuse was devastating, but God healed me by teaching forgiveness and the power of letting go of things outside of my control. God healed my mind and enabled me to fully depend on Him for everything.

Due to family genetics, I continue to take anti-depression medication. Asking God for wisdom and increased faith, I continue to face the monster of chronic disease as it slowly progresses. Medication, a healthful diet, moderate exercise, and adequate rest help.

Steve and I are still married and learning to love differently every day. Being together 24/7 since his retirement has challenges, but we're committed to our marriage and pray together for wisdom to love each other with God's love. We enjoy living near our son and his wife.

I have yet to publish my music, but it's still a possibility. It's in God's hands to direct me as to what to do with it and when. He is my life, my inspiration, and my song.

This memoir is not just my story—no more than your story is yours alone. Our lives are intertwined with many others revolving around One life for "In the beginning was God" (John 1:1). All of life from the beginning to the end of time is about God's love expressed through His Son, Jesus Christ, and the mighty works of His hands. It is His story.

All of creation exists for the single purpose to glorify Him. Given the choice, mankind continually separates itself from God through pride and self-gratification. Before creation, God prepared a way to reconcile man to Himself through His Son, Jesus Christ.

Our stories, yours and mine, are a mere stitch in the fabric of time intricately woven by the hand of God. To Him be the glory forever and ever.

> I consider everything a loss because of the surpassing worth of knowing Christ Jesus my Lord, for whose sake I have lost all things. I consider them garbage, that I may gain Christ and be found in him, not having a righteousness of my own that comes from the law, but that which is through faith in Christ–the righteousness that comes from God on the basis of faith.
>
> I want to know Christ–yes, to know the power of His resurrection and participation in His sufferings, becoming like Him in His death, and so, somehow, attaining the resurrection from the dead. Not that I have already obtained all this, or have already arrived at my goal, but I press on to take hold of that for which Christ Jesus took hold of me.
>
> Brothers and sisters, I do not consider myself yet to have taken hold of it. But one thing I do: Forgetting what is behind and straining toward what is ahead, I press on toward the goal to win the prize for which God has called me heavenward in Christ Jesus.
> – Philippians 3:10b-14 (NASB)

Vivien Chambers:

Faith and I started a rough draft of this book in 2000. So why did it take 24 years to complete? First, several of Faith's journals were missing, leaving numerous gaps in the story. Second, I became preoccupied with raising five children.

By the time we discussed revisiting the book ten or fifteen years later, Faith had matured so much, that past events felt surreal, compelling her to wonder if all this *actually* happened to her.

Yes, it absolutely did. I know, because she lassoed me into her turmoil. God invited me into her healing process even though I lacked formal education or training in psychology or spiritual healing. But God often uses the most unlikely people or "the foolish things of this world" for His purposes. This time He used both. His strength was displayed in my weakness.

It took two months of nearly daily prayer sessions for Faith to completely integrate. Previous therapy and constant reinforcement of truth prepared her for healing in God's perfect timing.

Several missing journals emerged in 2023 after Steve and Faith moved. This enabled us to finally complete her miraculous story of God's healing grace.

We pray that Faith's story inspired and, if needed, encouraged you to seek inner healing.

To God be the glory!

Acknowledgements

Many people took part in my healing. Without them healing may still be pending and there definitely wouldn't be this book.

First and foremost thank You, Jesus, for guiding our prayer sessions, for the visitations, and for healing me.
The staff members at Rapha who prayed for and with me, taught me truths of God's Word and helped me discover many of my repressed emotions. Eric, Brian, Peggy, Dr. Logan, Shawn, Betty, psyche techs, and even fellow "member," Rick, who drew out my repressed anger.
Dr. Kathy for all the years of helping me process a life of shame and grief.
Howard, for praying with me and helping me complete the race for inner healing.
Dan & Becky for supporting me and tolerating Daphne.
Paul for being available to offer prayer and guidance.
Vivien for hours of prayers and helping me tell my story.
Jenica for formatting this book.

My deepest gratitude to you all.
– Faith

Timeline

To share the extent of Faith's miraculous healing from DID, we've included a timeline derived from journal entries, memories, and other sources. Specific dates relating to Faith's father have deliberately been omitted.

1988
August
1: Suicidal thoughts
2: Dr. Kathy admits Faith into outpatient
3: 5 days Rapha outpatient
8: Rapha admission
Grievance letters to God & parents
October:
3: Home
4: Steve returns to work
November:
3: Josh's accident
7: Rapha day hospital
December 3: Discharge from day hospital

1992
June 27: Sunday looms ahead
1993
Letter to parents > vacation boundaries
August 30: Knee pain
October 10: Inner child

1994
July: Chronic disease symptoms

1995
Daddy died
Different voices
Alisa & Daphne emerge through imagery
Chronic disease diagnosis
October: Daphne enters hospital for suicidal thoughts, Safehouse for Daphne

1996
January 24: Faith's loud anointing during church service, Maymee emerges
February 12: God is going to heal me!
14: 'Roid Rage, Annie emerges
August 10: Maymee talks in group
December:
14: Told Vivien about MPD, The System
22: One Ear to TV
23: Daphne calls Dan, Daphne journals
25: Dolls for Christmas
27: Be Kind to Steve, Maymee journals
28: Daphne work
30: Session with Dr. Kathy related to Daphne's abuse

1997
January:
1: Daphne called Dan
4: Faith & Maymee journal
5: Maymee journals - Daphne returns to safe house
6: Maymee calls Vivien - prayer for young Daphne
7: Baby Daphne with Jesus
8: Daphne with Jesus, Faith & baby doll with Jesus
9: Annie meets Jesus
10: Attack! Fear of rejection
11: Prayer with Vivien: Daphne forgives parents
12: Daphne calls Vivien - Annie talks to Vivien, Vision
13: Annie's self-portrait
14: Rough couple of days, Prayer with Vivien
16: MLK practice, Vivien prays for Annie

19: Steve's dad died
20: MLK concert
21: Steve's dad's funeral, Joey & Jesus
24: Daphne's integration, Annie wants hugs
25: Maymee journals
26: Need to go to church to speak to Phyllis
27: "Mother beat baby Faith"
29: Nathan & Jesus
February:
12: Maymee & Nathan integrate
26: Janet & Jesus
27: Full Integration
March 4: Awareness of being a 41 yr old married woman
August:
5: Fear of church trip - declining health
26: Single personality
October 24: Letter to Maymee

2000
March: Howard
20: New pain medicine for chronic disease
22: I am not a disease
April
3: I want a Mt. Sinai experience
10: Anxious about upcoming session with Howard
May 31: Tom in Chronic Disease Bible study
December: Attack! New abuse memory

2001
January 9: Hospital for depression, permanent anti-depression medication

2002
January: Howard confronts Faith, PhD

February: Terri: We had one prayer session with Terri. We prayed for her alter "Nobody" whom Terri said had integrated. During the session, Terri mentioned she had been a victim of Satanic Ritual Abuse. When probing beyond Nobody's issues, Terri experienced an immediate severe headache. Lacking experience and unfamiliar with the extent of physical repercussions, the three of us agreed she might be safer in the hands of someone experienced in prayer counseling. Sadly, we lost contact with her and know nothing about her current mental health.

Works Cited

Mc Gee, Robert, *The Search for Significance, Seeing Your True Worth Through God's Eyes*, Nashville, Tennessee: Thomas Nelson, Inc, 1998, 2003

Anderson, Neil, *The Bondage Breaker, Overcoming Negative Thoughts, Irrational Feelings, Habitual Sins*, Eugene, Oregon: Harvest House Publishers, 2000, 2019

Davis, Truman C., "The Crucifixion of Jesus: The Passion of Christ from a Medical Point of View." (Originally published in Arizona Medical Association's Arizona Medicine, March 1965.)

Bible references were acquired from Blue Letter Bible at blueletterbible.org

About the Authors

Faith Alison lives a mentally, physically, and spiritually healthful lifestyle with her husband of forty-three years even though her chronic diseases are still ongoing. She enjoys spending time with her son and his wife and their fur-babies and grand-fur-babies. Her hobbies include learning Spanish, yoga, reading, composing music, arts and crafts, sewing, and gardening.

Vivien Chambers and her husband of forty-three years have five grown children and nine grandchildren. When not playing with her grandkids, she also enjoys water aerobics, listening to a wide variety of music, reading various genres, writing, and doing arts and crafts projects.

Made in United States
Orlando, FL
31 May 2024